the star
principle

the star principle

How It Can Make You Rich

RICHARD KOCH

PIATKUS

PIATKUS

First published in Great Britain in 2008 by Piatkus Books

Copyright © 2008 by Richard Koch

The moral right of the author has been asserted

A CIP catalogue record for this book
is available from the British Library

ISBN 978-0-7499-2840-7

Edited by Andrew John
Typeset in Bembo by Goldust Design
Printed and bound in Great Britain by Mackays of Chatham,
Chatham, Kent

Piatkus Books
An imprint of
Little, Brown Book Group
100 Victoria Embankment
London EC4Y 0DY

An Hachette Livre UK Company

www.piatkus.co.uk

For Matthew and Tocker,
with special thanks to Rhona and Charles

contents

acknowledgements

I have lived with the ideas for this book since I started working with the Boston Consulting Group (BCG), what seems a lifetime ago. The work is a fusion of my first life as a strategy consultant, my second as an entrepreneur and investor, and my third as an author. In one sense, therefore, I should thank my thousands of former colleagues and clients for their insights. Yet the idea of the star business, in all its stark magnificence, can be attributed to one person, Bruce Henderson, founder of BCG, and perhaps the most influential business thinker of all time. I had the uncertain privilege of knowing and talking to Bruce when he was an extremely Big Cheese and I was the most junior of colleagues; it was typical of Bruce that he would talk to anyone who was interested in his ideas, and although conversations with Bruce were always challenging he made you think very hard.

For helping me develop my ideas about star ventures I owe a great debt to my former partners, Iain Evans, Jim Lawrence, and Peter Johnson in LEK, and Robin Field, Anthony Rice, Nick Dodd, and Jamie Reeve in SVP.

The idea for the book came from discussions with Nicholas Brealey and Sally Lansdell; all power to them. Fiona Lindsay did a terrific job as agent for this book and its predecessor, assisted by the excellent Mary Bekhait.

Thanks also to my wonderful 'editorial committee' of friends – Mary saxe Falstein, Martin Nye, Robin Field, Jamie Reeve, Peter Johnson, Rick Haller, Chris Outram, Anthony Rice, Chris Eyles, Graham Ross Russell and Matthew Grimsdale. Douglas Blowers created the illustrations with great skill and, as always, Aaron Calder provided essential all-round help. At Piatkus, Alan Brooke and Denise Dwyer have been a joy to work with.

Finally, thanks to all the entrepreneurs who made all this possible, in particular David Collischon, Robin Field, André Plisnier, Denis Blais, John Murphy, Charles Rolls, Andrew Black, Edward Wray, Iain Evans and Jim Lawrence. Several of these commented on the text and André, David and Charles went to extraordinary lengths to ensure that the pieces on their companies were accurate. All inadequacies are, beyond doubt, entirely mine.

I must create a system or be enslaved
by another man's.
I will not reason and compare;
my business is to create.

WILLIAM BLAKE

One cannot resist the invasion of ideas.

VICTOR HUGO

introduction

La Dolce Vita for You?

I n the late 1990s, Andrew Black, known as Bert to his friends, had an idea. As a former professional gambler, he liked nothing more than playing poker through the night, and the thing he liked most about poker, apart from winning, was that the game was free. There were no bookmakers around to slice off their huge margin. Collectively, the friends he played with broke even. If one lost, somebody else won. But, when it came to horseracing and other sports, there was no way that individuals could exchange bets or avoid paying a king's ransom to third-party bookies.

Unless Bert did something about it. Which he did. Together with the brother of a friend, Bert started a 'betting exchange' called Betfair. A betting exchange acts as a broker between individuals, charging a very small commission for doing so, a tiny fraction of what the bookies charge when they set the odds.

Betfair was started in September 2000 with about £1 million dredged up from friends and family – no venture capitalist would invest in it. By the start of 2001, Betfair was a tiny business that was running out of cash fast. Despite its precarious prospects, and its failure to make much headway in the betting world, I was delighted to invest £1.5 million in Betfair. I didn't need to think much about it, because Betfair was a particular type of business, one that the Boston Consulting Group terms a 'star business'.

(I'll explain in the next two chapters what a star business is. Just trust me for the moment – you can easily recognise a star business when you see one, and starting one is quite possible, too, if you know exactly what you are aiming for.)

Why should you care about this? Because today Bert Black and his co-founder, Ed Wray, have each made several hundred million pounds from Betfair, and it may well eventually make them billionaires; and because I struck gold, too, even though I was not a founder or even a founding investor. My first investment – a few months after the company started – has multiplied 53 times. In total I've made more than £100 million from Betfair.

Betfair is not an isolated example. I've made four other investments in star businesses, only one of which I co-founded and worked in. I've made millions out of each one, in total 10 times what I put in (the simple average was sixteen times). The founders profited more. Even ordinary employees made out like bandits. We all benefited hugely from being involved in the early days with a star business.

Why should you care? Because you too can make a lot of money and have great fun, just by doing the same. Whether you want to start a firm or not, whether or not you have savings to invest, a star business can make your life much sweeter, richer in every way. Let me repeat: this applies even if you are a normal employee, not an entrepreneur or a moneybags.

You could stop reading here. You could pass up the

chance to transform your life. Maybe you don't need or want a richer life. But I'll make you two promises, which I'll keep.

1. This book is easy to read and assumes no special knowledge about business.

2. If you act on what I say, your magical mystery tour of the star world will make you more confident, more useful and a lot wealthier.

part one
the idea

1

What will make you successful?

To know much is not to be wise.
Euripides

Imagine that there was a business you could work in, where you would be somebody important; where you could have *several times* the influence and fun that you could expect in a normal firm; where you would be paid more, get great bonuses and perhaps qualify for free shares that could become valuable.

Imagine that there was a foolproof formula for making your money grow, so that, each time you put it to work, it more than doubled! Imagine you'd stand a good chance of multiplying your money ten times, with an outside chance you'd hit the jackpot and reap a reward 100 times your investment.

Wouldn't you go out of your way to invest or work in a business like that?

Pure fantasy? A fairy story? Life doesn't give you breaks like that.

Or does it? My contention, preposterous as it sounds, is

that it does. There *is* a magic formula. There *is* a way to get *several times* more money and fun out of a business.

By finding a star venture.

What is a star venture? It has two qualities. One, it operates in a high-growth market. Two, it is the leader in that market. (In the next chapter I'll explain much more about star ventures. Very few people understand what star ventures are, which is good, because it makes it easier for people who *do* understand to find them!)

Look at the evidence. In my five star businesses, my *total* return has been *ten times* the money I put in and the simple average has been *16 times*.

None of the star investments has failed. The *lowest* return was just over double my money. Three gave me back more than *15 times* my starting cash. One gave me *24 times*. The best gave me *53 times* the first part of my investment and an absolute return of £26.4 million for that first part. The total value of the deal (my share was 7.4 per cent) was £1.54 *billion*, for a company that only ever raised £2.5 million.

OK, I have also made some mistakes – but by investing in businesses that were not stars. Even including my blunders and disappointments, however, my average return has been *six times* the cash put at risk.

Star ventures have made me rich. But enough about me. Let's talk about you.

What determines your success?

Whether you are an entrepreneur, an employee or an investor in a new or young venture, there is one overwhelming answer that nearly everyone does not know or act on. If you know the answer and act on it, your life is transformed.

Is it *your ability*?

No, it is not your ability. I have known outstandingly able people who have started a new business and failed. Sometimes two or three new ventures that went bust. I have terrifically talented friends who've worked in small firms, and never achieved great results. I've known very bright and experienced investors who've never made much above the average.

And I have known many people of average ability who have been extraordinarily successful. Most of the people I backed in new ventures were bright, personable and dedicated. But they did not succeed because of these qualities. To be honest, they were no better and no worse than many people who have achieved little.

Is it how *hard you work*?

No, it is not. Most people in a new venture work long hours. They put their heart and soul into the business. As employees, they are often paid less and work harder than in larger firms where they worked before and could work again. And more than 95 per cent of these people are not particularly successful.

When I've invested in a venture and see people there working all the hours God sends, I know it's in trouble. If it needs that much dedication and overwork, it's because it could not survive without it.

When I've put money into a new company and see the boss with his feet up and the employees quietly confident and chatting freely to each other about some trivia, do I get annoyed? No. It makes me confident. These people are delivering their numbers and yet they are relaxed. There's some slack in the system. The business is working.

Is it having the right *mix of people*?

There is something to the idea that most new ventures fail because they don't have the right balance between the optimist and the pessimist, the person who has the vision and puts her foot down on the accelerator, and the person who has her feet on the ground and can stamp on the brake when money is tight or something foolish is being attempted. There is something to the idea that all new businesses need a visionary (the entrepreneur), a technical person who is expert at what the business does (the doer), and someone to organise the people and run the show (the manager). No new venture will succeed without the right mix of people.

Yet this is not the determining factor. Many ventures have a good balance of people and yet don't grow to any substantial size. And most of those I've worked and invested in – the ultra-successful, the successful, the mediocre, and those that went belly up – have struggled to find the right mix of people. But every one has got there eventually, if necessary from my banging heads together, firing the boss or bringing in the missing person.

Conflict between founders and employees, and between employees, is endemic in small business. It's inevitable. And probably a good thing. Show me a venture team you say has always been 100 per cent happy, harmonious and balanced and there are only two possibilities: one is that you are deluded; the other that the business is going nowhere. If all the team's energy is going into getting on with each other, there will be compromise on key decisions and no zest left to deal with difficult customers and competitors.

Is the key to success the *people you select* as partners and early employees – the sheer quality of the individuals?

This is a tempting thesis. It's one that the venture-capital community – who get most things right – agree with unanimously. The common cliché among venture capitalists is that there are three reasons for success: people, people, and people. And, although it's a cliché, I don't know any venture capitalist who doesn't really believe it.

Could all these money makers be wrong? No and yes.

Within the great majority of ventures, the main difference between success and failure is indeed the people. Most ventures start off on the wrong tack and find their niche only because the founders and employees experiment relentlessly until they find a formula that works. They triumph through trial and error, if they don't run out of cash first. So the venture capitalists are right. In a poorly positioned business – the great majority of ventures – the people make the difference between success and failure.

True, but largely beside the point. There is a better way to succeed than relying on the qualities of the people, which in any case are difficult to know from the outside and without hindsight.

The answer is not to work or invest in the great majority of ventures. The key is to select the ventures that are likely to succeed anyway. Without superhuman people. Without perfect balance between the skills of the people. Without blood, toil, tears and sweat. Without the need to keep chopping and changing before the correct formula emerges.

The useful answer is not 'people, people, people'. The

really potent, consistently successful answer is '*positioning, positioning, positioning*'.

Provided the positioning truly is exceptional. Provided the venture is a star business.

When you found a star business, when you are an early employee in a star business, when you invest in a star business, you are setting the odds in your favour. You are very likely to prosper. What is the shortcut to success? It is the star business.

We all like to believe that our triumphs come from our consummate skill, whereas failure, of course, is due to other people or sheer bad luck. Success in a poorly positioned business, against the odds, may indeed be the result of your fantastic abilities. But why make obstacles to overcome? Why not remove the obstacles to success and use the launch pad for success? Why not get involved with a star venture?

Having the idea for a star business takes imagination. Validating the idea of a star business – checking that the business really is a star as properly defined – requires some combination of hard thinking, research and experimentation. Launching a star business requires the same amount of courage and determination as launching any other venture. Finding someone else's star business takes a reasonable amount of care. Yet none of these actions requires exceptional intelligence or creativity. They require normal levels of skills, plus the knowledge easily gleaned from this book. Naturally, if you are exceptionally smart that is a bonus. But not a necessity.

All together now. What will make you successful?

Positioning will. A star business will. In terms of improving the odds, nothing else comes close.

2

So what exactly is a star business?

The star of the portfolio is a rare and wonderful thing; its value is also rarely recognised and, typically, it is strategically mismanaged.

Bruce D. Henderson

Since star businesses are so wonderful to work in or invest in, it's clearly crucial to know what they look like. You don't need to know anything about business besides what we cover in this chapter. In fact, it is better to know *nothing* else about business and to understand thoroughly what a star business is, than it is to have the knowledge that most people have about business – from working in it for decades or from doing an MBA – and *not to know* what a star business is. So, whether you are a total novice or the most experienced director around, once you understand about star businesses, you will know the *one thing* that is most vital for success.

And it's easy to understand.

A star business has two attributes:

★ it is the leader in its market niche; and

★ the market niche is growing fast, at least 10 per cent a year.

A star business is the leader in its market niche

To be the leader simply means that it is bigger *in the niche* than any other firm. We measure size by sales value (also known as *revenues* or *turnover*). If the venture has sales of $1 million and there is nobody whose sales in the same niche reach $1 million, then it is the leader. Note that 'leadership' is objectively defined by sales, and has nothing to do with competing claims about 'being the best' or being most highly rated by customers, which are difficult to judge and not as important anyway. The thing that matters most is how customers in the niche vote with their money.

Has a question just popped up in your mind? 'Ah,' you may say, 'but how do you define what the market niche is?' That is indeed a profound question, and I will answer it with several examples throughout the book. It is possible to get the definition of the niche wrong – as I sometimes have. But the basic idea is very simple. *For a niche to be a separate market, it must have different customers, different products or services and a different way of doing business* from the main market or other market niches. Finally, the *ranking of competitors is different* in a valid market niche – the leader in the niche is different from the leader in the main market. If there is no difference in how competitors fare in the niche versus the main market, the niche is not really different.

For 70 years, until the 1980s, there was no dispute that the leading world car manufacturers were Ford, General Motors and Chrysler (the 'Big Three'). Yet alongside the main car market there evolved a market in smaller, cheaper cars. The most successful were the Volkswagen and later the Mini. The small-car market was a separate niche. It had different customers (Europeans, and those on a tighter budget), different products and different market leaders.

Sports cars are another separate segment. The customers are different from those in the main market (richer, more interested in performance and image, sometimes younger). The products are markedly different. A host of different competitors sprang up in the market for sports cars, with Porsche and Mazda proving the long-term winners, and the Big Three almost nowhere.

The sports-car market itself evolved, with high-price, super-performance marques becoming clearly distinct from 'ordinary' sports cars. Take marques such as Ferrari and Maserati. Their customers are more affluent or fanatical than regular sports-car owners. Their products are hand-crafted, not mass-manufactured. They have their own mystique, great design, super-powerful engines, acceleration and road holding that can (depending on the driver's skill) be death-defying. The cheapest new Ferrari costs much more than a top-of-the-line Porsche. The super-performance marques *are* separate market niches. For a time at least they were all star businesses, each firm having leadership in its niche.

The car market has branched out into a large number

of other separate niches – for example, minivans, where Chrysler leads; the luxury segment, headed by Mercedes-Benz; and the sports–utility (4x4) niche, where there is yet another leader, Jeep.

How far can this 'separate niche' game be taken? Could we decide, if we wanted, to become the market leader in making yellow cars and make that a new star business? Well, no. Yellow cars are not a sufficiently different product from cars of other colours, and just painting all our cars yellow is not a sufficiently different way of doing business. Sufficiently different from what? you may ask. Sufficiently different from how all other car manufacturers conduct their business. Sufficiently different to enable us to have lower costs, or higher prices, than competitors. Sufficiently different from what Ford and General Motors do anyway – they are not going to stop making yellow cars just because we proclaim them to be our speciality. Sufficiently different to attract a whole new set of customers, or to make yellow car sales grow faster than white or red ones.

Are diet cola drinks a separate niche market? Imagine that you had the idea of making low–calorie cola long before Coke or Pepsi. Could you have made a separate niche market out of it? Could Koch Lite Kola have been a new star?

Just possibly. Diet cola appeals, largely, to different customers. But whether that appeal is sufficiently strong to overcome all the advantages that Coke and Pepsi have – their strong brands, loyal customers, proprietary distribution systems and huge economies of scale in making and marketing soft drinks – is highly dubious. Coke and Pepsi saw the potential before anybody else. Even if Koch Lite Kola had been the first of its kind, it would soon have been swamped by Diet Coke and Pepsi Lite. Low-calorie cola is just too similar to regular cola, and the world's top two cola brands are just too strong.

What if we had made a different kind of soft drink, something not a cola, with a unique taste? Could that have been a star? Why, yes. Step forward, Dr Pepper.

Nothing else tastes like it. Neither Coke nor Pepsi has ever been able to construct a viable rival to Dr Pepper, which still has 100 per cent of the Dr Pepper niche market. (Dr Pepper was actually launched in 1885, a year *before* Coca-Cola. In 1965, a mere four-score years later, Coke test-marketed 'Chime' to take on Dr Pepper. Chime sank without trace.)

The proof of the pudding is the ranking of competitors' market shares. A firm has a separate market niche if it is number one in the niche market. It has sustainable niche leadership if it can hang on to that number-one position, against actual or possible competition from the leader in the main market.

Dr Pepper is still the leader in the Dr Pepper niche, and nobody else is anywhere.

Red Bull is another case. In America and Europe, Red Bull invented the 'energy drink' category. All attempts by the Coca-Cola Corporation and other soft-drink makers to compete with Red Bull have failed. Energy drinks are a separate niche and Red Bull is a valuable star.

There is another clue as to whether or not a niche market is viable, and it is simply this: is the niche highly profitable? Does it generate a lot of cash? Leadership in a niche is not valuable unless, sooner or later, the niche is very profitable and gushes out cash. For sure, if your product is very good and you give it away, you can attain leadership in a niche. Free newspapers, for example. But unless you have some other way of taking in cash – through advertising in this case – your niche business will be unprofitable and gobble up cash.

It follows that you can tell whether or not niche leadership really exists by seeing whether the niche leader is very profitable and cash-positive. If not, there is a kind of theoretical niche leadership, but the niche has little or no practical value. It will never qualify as a star business. Is Dr Pepper's niche leadership valuable? Is Red Bull's? You bet!

If you're clear about niche leadership, you're most of the way to understanding how to identify a star business. Remember, there is a second condition that must be satisfied, and it's quite a tough condition – but simple to understand!

The market niche must be growing fast

A venture is not a star unless the niche where it operates is growing by at least 10 per cent a year. More precisely, the niche must grow at least 10 per cent a year, on average, over the next five years, and preferably for decades.

Why is growth important? Because the power of compound arithmetic is such that, in a high-growth venture, sales – and profits, when they appear – will multiply quickly. It is quite different from the great majority of firms, which grow only slowly, and where profit growth is difficult and far from automatic.

A business with sales of $10 million that grows at 3 per cent a year – roughly the rate the economy grows – will increase by 34 per cent over a decade, to just over $13 million. What will a business that grows at 30 per cent a year – ten times 3 per cent – grow by in the same time? You might assume is it ten times 34 per cent, which is 340 per cent, and add a bit for the effect of compounding, to take the growth to perhaps 500 per cent. If this were true the sales after ten years would have grown to $50 million. But the correct answer is nearly $138 million. Such is the magic of compound interest, which Albert Einstein called 'the most powerful force in the universe'.

Note that we are talking about *future* growth. Of course, nobody can be sure how fast any market niche will grow, particularly over a long time. But a good guide to future growth is past growth and the trend in past growth. When I invested in Betfair it was tiny, but its market niche was growing at more than 30 per cent a *month*. It didn't take a genius to work out that future growth would outstrip the required 10 per cent a *year*.

Clearly, the faster the growth, the better. Because of compound arithmetic, a market niche that is growing at 20 per cent a year is more than twice as good as one growing at 10 per cent a year, and a market growing at 50 per cent a year is more than five times as good. In fact, over a mere ten years, and forgetting about the future beyond that, a 50 per cent growth market is more than 22 times as good as one growing at 10 per cent. Because Betfair was growing so fast, I knew that, disasters aside (and there could easily have been disasters), it would end up as a very large business. I marvel now that other people could not see that. But, when you see a struggling, loss-making venture fast running out of cash, it requires a lot of imagination or faith in stars to believe that this puny acorn would become a mighty oak. In that failure of imagination lies our opportunity.

Why do we take the growth rate of the market niche, rather than the growth of the new venture itself? Because the latter is affected not just by market growth but also by whether it is gaining or losing market share within the niche. It is vital that a star business should at least maintain its lead over its nearest competitor in the niche, and highly desirable for the venture to increase its lead. But this is a separate consideration from the niche market growth, and it is simpler and clearer to start with that.

Why is a star business so attractive?

It is the *combined effect* of niche leadership and high niche growth that makes a star venture so wonderful. Leadership means that the company and its products are preferred by the niche's customers. The business should therefore be more profitable than one that's not a leader. A leading firm should have higher prices, or lower costs, than a similar business that is a follower. Why higher prices? Because the customers prefer the product. Why lower costs? Because the firm can spread its fixed costs over a much greater volume of business than competitors can. Upshot: a leader should be very profitable, and, the further the venture is ahead of its competitors in the niche, the more profitable it should be.

To have a valuable firm in the future, whatever its size and profitability today, all you need is leadership in a fast-growth niche. Provided the firm is tolerably well run, leadership will make the firm profitable and cash-positive. Growth will make it big. If you grasp these two ideas, you will have huge insight into the future. That is all it takes to find a wonderful place to work or to put your hard-earned cash.

Are there pitfalls for a star venture?

Only one, but it's huge. The trap is that a star stops being a star by losing leadership in its niche. If that happens, a venture worth a fortune can suddenly become almost worthless.

The danger is acute. There is a considerable chance that a star business will forfeit its leadership. How come? Because when a market is growing fast, a firm can continue to grow and yet lose market share to a rival. There is so much market available that a star may not even notice the danger. But suddenly a rival can become bigger, and that is nearly always fatal to the value of the erstwhile star. If you are aware of the danger, however, a star can normally fight off a challenger.

How rare are stars?

There can be only one market leader (or perhaps two co-leaders), but there can be many followers in a market niche. For new ventures, perhaps one in four is a genuine niche leader.

Few market niches grow at least 10 per cent a year. For big, established companies, typically only 5 per cent or fewer of their products grow this fast. For smaller, newer ventures, the odds are not as bad. I estimate that about 15–25 per cent of new enterprises' market positions are growing annually by at least 10 per cent.

So, roughly one in four new ventures is a niche leader, and one in five is growing at the rate required of a star. Multiply these two probabilities together. Of the 20 per cent that are growing fast enough, roughly a quarter – 5 per cent of the total – are likely to be stars. About 1 in 20 start-ups is a star.

So stars are rare. But they are not so rare that, with a bit of patience and careful thought, you can't discover one – or create one yourself. If you look intelligently for a star, you will find it.

Where did the idea of a star business come from?

I'm fascinated by the history of this idea, which also tells us why the idea is not used more. But, if you just want to benefit from the star idea and couldn't care two hoots about its heritage, then skip the rest of this chapter.

There is a branch of business theory called *strategy*, which was invented by a new consulting firm, the Boston Consulting Group (BCG), in the 1960s. BCG's most famous invention was the growth/share matrix, which says there are four types of business from a strategic view-point:

★ **stars**: leaders in high-growth markets;

★ **question marks**: followers in high-growth markets;

★ **cash cows**: leaders in low-growth markets; and

★ **dogs**: followers in low-growth markets.

BCG drew the growth/share matrix as illustrated in Figure 2.1:

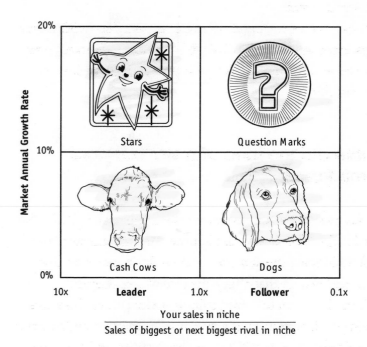

Figure 2.1 Relative market share

BCG also drew up prescriptions for what to do with business in each box, as we can see in Figure 2.2. When I worked at BCG in the mid-1970s, these were the rules of thumb.

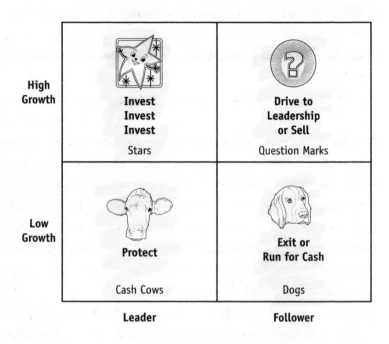

Figure 2.2 Rules of thumb

The two boxes we should focus on are the star quadrant, of course, but also the question-mark box. The rule for stars is to invest, invest, invest – do whatever it takes to remain a star, maintaining leadership in the niche, and if possible increasing the lead over rivals. At BCG we promised our clients that they would never regret any actions or expenditure to protect and enhance the leadership positions enjoyed by their stars. We knew how valuable these positions would be in the future if they held on to clear leadership. Equally, we knew how much money would be flushed away if a star lost its premier status.

Question marks are, of course, the other side of the star coin. For every leader in a fast-growth market there is a follower, and there are usually several. The dilemma of the number two in a fast-growth niche – the question mark in the strongest position to challenge the star – is quite acute.

Should the number two throw everything into the pot to challenge the star venture, to try to overtake it and replace it as the leader? To do so is usually very difficult and expensive, and the effort may not succeed. Of course, if it does succeed, if it overtakes the current star, the number two becomes the number one – it ends up with a very valuable star business. But, if the effort fails, the question mark will have used up a tremendous amount of cash and talent in a vain cause – with nothing to show for it. That cash, almost certainly, has vanished for ever.

BCG advised great selectivity for question-mark positions, telling clients to go one way or the other. For a few question marks, try to drive to dominance, to become the leader. For most of the question marks, sell the business, and let someone else waste their cash. The dilemma of the question mark was, of course, the reason for its name.

Why isn't the idea of the star business more popular?

In the late 1970s, the growth/share matrix was heavily criticised and fell out of favour. The main reason was guilt by association. BCG came up with the matrix as part of a dastardly plot to allocate resources centrally. In the quest to give head office, its planners and its consultants something to do, the matrix was used to set strategy from the top, to take funds from certain divisions and allocate them to other divisions. The idea of central planning was cumbersome and, in most cases, daft. It rightly caused a strong negative reaction from those running businesses. Rather than defend the matrix and the centralising system it represented, BCG chose to emphasise its other ideas and products.

They threw the baby out with the bathwater. At the level of individual niche markets, the ideas behind the matrix were incredibly useful. When I wrote a book on strategy in 1995, I revived the use of the growth/share matrix for small businesses and business units within large firms. I met a hugely favourable response, and to my knowledge everyone who has tried to use my approach, built around the early BCG ideas, has found it practical and useful.[1] Still, my one-man crusade to revive BCG's early ideas has only caused a few ripples on the surface of the business world.

When it comes to investment, there are very few people in that world who understand classical strategy concepts, especially the rather old ones that I am using. As far as I know, there is no private-equity or other investment firm specifically targeting star ventures. I hope that lasts. Let's keep the value of star enterprises a secret between you and me!

---

[1] Richard Koch (2006), *The Financial Times Guide to Strategy* (London: Pearson), is the third, updated edition. It is a guide to the whole of strategy, both for individual business units and for corporations. Entrepreneurs interested in strategy can find an even more detailed step-by-step guide in Richard Koch and Peter Nieuwenhuizen (2006), *Simply Strategy* (London: Pearson). Accompanying software is available to take your firm's data and construct all the strategy displays you could possibly want!

3

The power of the star idea

Ideas shape the course of history.
John Maynard Keynes

'm not the only entrepreneur or investor who's benefited from star businesses. Virtually every share in the public markets that has made people a fortune – excepting only special situations such as mining – has been a star business, that is, a niche leader in a high-growth market.

Google was and is a star business. Google is many times bigger than any other search engine. It was founded only in 1998 and already processes more than 91 million search requests a day. The market is still doubling in size every year. Not surprisingly, Google is a fantastically valuable star, worth $123 billion as I write.

Amazon was and is a star business. It is the largest online bookseller by a wide margin. Including other products, Amazon's revenues in 2005 were $8.5 billion and its current market value is $13.5 billion.

Netscape, founded in 1994, quickly became the star player in the Web-browser market. Netscape was sold to AOL in

1999 for $4.2 billion. The deal was great for Netscape's founder, Jim Clark, and terrible for AOL. Before long Microsoft's Explorer browser had obliterated Netscape's position.

eBay is the star of person-to-person e-tailing (selling on the net) and e-payments, both huge markets, as well as the star in its original online auction business. Founded in 1995, eBay now has over 180 million users and is valued on the stock market at a staggering $39 billion, which means each user is reckoned to be worth nearly $217!

Yahoo! started business in 1995 as a search and portal site and has added communities and media-rich content along the way. Most of its businesses are stars. Worth $35 billion, it has more than 400 million users.

Specialist, user-generated-content e-networks afford terrific scope for star businesses. For example, less than two years after it started, MySpace was bought by News Corporation for $580 million in 2005, while Facebook's backers think it is worth between $8 billion and $10 billion.

Skype, which lets Internet users talk to friends online free, is another great instant star. In 1995, two years after it started, it was sold to eBay for $2.6 billion. Skype now has more than 100 million users, aged on average just under 30.

Just over 20 years ago, thanks largely to a deal with IBM, Microsoft became the leader in software for PCs, a very fast-growth market. At the time it took niche leadership and became a star, Microsoft was worth almost nothing. Now it's the world's top software company, valued at $271 billion.

It was not until the 1990s that biotechnology companies

appeared viable. Since then, the market has mushroomed, and two biotech niche leaders, Amgen and Genentech, are each worth about $83 billion.

Even further back, Intel, founded in 1968, rapidly became by far the world's largest semiconductor maker, with a current market share in PC microprocessors of 80 per cent. For decades this was a very fast-growth business, making Intel a star. Even today, Intel is growing its sales and profits at more than 10 per cent a year. At times Intel was close to bankruptcy and its shares were on the floor. But its star status was vindicated and it's now worth $115 billion.

Probably the first quoted technology company was US Steel in 1901, after it acquired Carnegie Steel, another star business, then the world's largest steel producer. That deal, then the largest personal commercial transaction in US history, netted Andrew Carnegie (1835–1919), a poor Scottish immigrant to the United States in 1848, $480 million. That was an awesome sum at the time – more than 1 per cent of all US wealth.

Not long after, Henry Ford started a new star business, taking the lead in the automobile niche. Ford's car plant at Highland Park, Detroit, opened on the first day of 1910. For many years Ford became the fastest-growing and most valuable star business around, second in value only to US Steel. Between 1910 and 1920 the number of Americans owning cars soared from under half a million to more than eight million – most of them Fords.

Star businesses needn't be anything to do with technology. Only one of my five stars is a technology venture. The longest-running star business is surely the Coca-Cola

Company, incorporated in 1888 and a consistent star business until the 1990s. For over a century, despite two world wars, the stock market crash of 1929 and the ensuing Great Depression, Coca-Cola remained a star. The global market for cola increased on trend by more than 10 per cent every year and Coke remained the dominant player in that market.

The value of the company increased with remarkable consistency, even bucking the trend and rising from 1929 to 1945. The company used World War Two to its immense advantage. After Pearl Harbor, Coke boss Robert Woodruff pledged to 'see that every man in uniform gets a bottle of Coca-Cola for five cents, wherever he is and whatever it costs our company'. The US administration exempted Coca-Cola that was sold to the military from all sugar rationing. The US Army gave Coke employees installing plants behind the front lines the pseudo-military status of 'technical observers'. These 'Coca-Cola Colonels' were exempt from the draft but actually wore Army uniforms and carried military rank according to their company salaries. General Eisenhower, a self-confessed Coke addict, cabled urgently from North Africa on 29 June, 1943: 'On early convoy request shipment three million bottled Coca-Cola (filled) and complete equipment for bottling, washing, capping same quantity twice monthly . . .'[2]

Coke became familiar throughout Europe during the war and continued its remarkably cosy arrangement with the US military in Germany and Japan during the postwar

[2] Quoted in Mark Pendergrast (1993), *For God, Country and Coca-Cola: The Unauthorized History of the Great American Soft Drink and the Company that Makes It* (London: George Weidenfeld and Nicolson), p. 203. Future references to Coca-Cola rely heavily on this source.

occupation. From the 1950s, Coke rode the wave of inter-
nationalisation. Roberto Goizueta, the CEO from 1980 to
1997, created more wealth for shareholders than any other
CEO in history. He became the first CEO who was not a
founder to become a billionaire. The business now rates a
value of $104 billion.

McDonald's is one of the great stars of business. In 1940
Dick and Mac McDonald opened a coffee shop in San
Bernardino, California. The business started to fly in 1948,
when they introduced their 'speedee service system', a
streamlined assembly line for hamburgers, giving the world
a new kind of restaurant, the fast-food hamburger shop.
Between 1948, when they started, and 1954, the McDonald
brothers opened eight highly successful restaurants. They
pioneered the limited menu and highly automated,
consistent food delivery that has been the backbone of
McDonald's success right up to today. They created a star
business, one that grew rapidly. They did well enough, but
failed to see the vast potential of their innovation. The
man who made McDonald's one of the most valuable stars
on the planet was Ray Kroc, who persuaded the brothers
to let him take charge of franchising the restaurants in
1955. Seeing the huge potential, Kroc bought the brothers
out in 1961 for $2.7 million. Today, McDonald's is the
world's largest chain of fast-food restaurants, with 447,000
employees serving nearly 50 million customers a day, and
over $20 billion sales. For the past 20 years the growth of
McDonald's has slowed and the business is now a 'cash
cow' rather than a star. Still, it is worth some $48 billion,
which is 17,778 *times* the price paid by Kroc.

More than four times as valuable as McDonald's is

Wal–Mart, the world's largest retailer. Some 60 years ago, the legendary Sam Walton made it into a star. By the time he was 40, in the early 1960s, he had one star business under his belt, having become the biggest independent variety-store operator. Walton then decided to start another star business – discount stores in small American towns. The first opened in 1962, at St Robert, Missouri. Wal–Mart remained a star for four decades, up to the 1990s. Today it's a cash cow worth $205 billion, making the Waltons one of the richest families on the planet.

Encyclopaedia Britannica remained a hugely valuable star business for decades, before suddenly succumbing to Microsoft's Encarta, and, more recently, the online Wikipedia, which is a star business waiting to happen. Wikipedia is used by 50 million people every day and growing at more than 100 per cent a year. Although not yet a for-profit business, it is potentially worth billions of dollars.

The pattern goes on and on. IKEA furniture, budget airlines such as Southwest and, in Europe, Ryanair and easyJet, the Sony Walkman, Yamaha and Honda motorcycles, Club Med, American Express, Federal Express, the Apple Mac and Apple iPod, 3M, Toys 'R' Us, Schwab brokerage, Intuit's Quicken financial software, Office Depot, Nike, Dell Computer Corporation, Auto Trader, Reuters – all these owned businesses that were, for a time, classic star businesses, throwing off enormous amounts of cash. Of course, stars set. Some lost ground to competitors, and suffered accordingly. Some remained leaders in their business when the market growth slowed, and became valuable 'cash cows'.

It is scarcely an exaggeration to say that every significant innovation, every new product and service that made it into the world and multiplied greatly, gave rise to a star business. And those stars that held their position for a long time have been responsible for creating the greatest wealth individuals have ever known.

Cities and city-states can also make themselves into valuable stars, almost invulnerable to challengers. In the mid-1990s, Sheik Mohammed decided to create a new fast-growth position for Dubai as *the* leading resort and holiday destination in the Middle East. Dubai City is now three times bigger in size and population, expanding further into both desert and sea. Up to 2002, only Arabs could buy freeholds. Now Europeans, Americans, Russians, Chinese, Indians and Japanese investors buy apartments or villas off plan, as soon as a project is announced. Branson, Beckham, consulates and foreign rulers snap up the newly created bijou islands. As long as Dubai continues to invest in further infrastructure – a monorail and new six-runway airport have been started – it is impossible for any neighbouring country such as Bahrain or Oman to catch up. Dubai has a ten-year lead in facilities and foreign investment, and it has a unique niche in customers' minds. The Dubai 'brand' makes it a secure star. Yet up to 1995 the market niche did not exist and many other countries could have built a similar position.

I've been an enthusiast of the star idea for the past 30 years. It's never failed me. As far as I know, it has never failed any of the hundreds of people I've introduced to it.

I still find it extraordinary. How can one idea be the source of most identifiable wealth creation, with the sole exception of natural resources? How can it be true that, for companies lucky enough to own star businesses, it is the stars, usually a small fraction of total revenues, that bring home most of the company's cash, and sometimes more than 100 per cent of it? How can a small number of star businesses reliably create such stupendous riches? How is it that the great majority of products, and companies, consume enormous amounts of sweat, tears, toil and cash, and give so little back? How is it that most people work so hard going nowhere much, while the few super-charged star ventures create so much with so little?

Yet it is so. Stars are where the universe creates good fortune. Stars are the source of wealth. Stars are the place to invest. Stars are the place to work.

Know only one thing, so that you can't ever forget it. Know the power of stars. Believe it. Act on it.

Once you know this one thing, all the rest of your professional life is tactics – how to find your star before anybody else, how to ensure it stays a star, how to work in a star as one of the early star-mongers, how to get the most out of your star. These tactics are what the rest of this book is all about. But the tactics depend upon believing in the star idea. Believe in it, because it is true, because it is the single most vital truth in the business world, and because it can set you free.

4

Stars are for everyone

There are no passengers on spaceship earth.
We are all crew.
Marshall McLuhan

My message, you will have gathered, is that, if you understand the idea of a star business, you can change your whole life.

'But that doesn't apply to me,' people I meet often say, 'because I don't have any spare money, and I don't have what it takes to become an entrepreneur.'

'It doesn't matter,' I always reply. 'Do you work for a living?'

'Yes.'

'Then it applies to you. You can change your life by working in a star venture.'

'Why would I want to do that? What difference would it make?'

'Because working in a star business is much more fun and you will earn much more money.'

'*Why?*'

'Well, before long, if not already, a star business will be coining money hand over fist. It can afford to be generous. It will reward loyalty and skill much more than an ordinary firm. It will be successful. And there is nothing in business – I know from first-hand experience – that's so much fun as working in a burgeoning, hugely successful small venture. It's easy to be a star in a star. It's easy to get promoted. It's easy to get fat bonuses. And, if you get a few shares or share options, you may end up with a surprisingly large nest egg. Even more important, you get a massive high from accomplishing something, from changing a market, from thrilling customers, from being a key part of a winning team.

'It doesn't stop there. Scrape some cash together and invest in a star business, and you'll likely multiply your money. Take your "winnings" and invest in another star. Before long, you'll be rich.

'It is *so much better to work in a star business*, rather than in a non-star business. Somewhere between 95 and 99 per cent of businesses are not stars, so the chances are that you're not working in one now. Think how much better life would be if you found a star to work in.

'It would be even better if you were one of the very early employees in a star business. *There is tremendous value and satisfaction in being one of the first twenty people in a new firm – being, believe it or not, a real entrepreneur.*'

The many-headed entrepreneur

The idea of the entrepreneur has rightly come under scrutiny recently. Writers such as Michael Gerber have pointed to the 'myth' that entrepreneurs are usually good at running businesses. True, but this critique doesn't go far enough.

The real myth of the entrepreneur is that there is always, or even usually, one key person in every new venture. Much more often, there are *several* people propelling a new business forward. Unless a business remains essentially the vehicle of the founder – and usually therefore very small – its business idea and character derive from the interactions of up to 20 early employees.

I see two roles in making a new business successful. On the one hand, there is the founder, or, more usually two, three or four founders. They get the business going. On the other hand, there are the first 12–20 employees. The interactions within the founders and early employees determine the character of the firm. The founders and first employees are, in my book, all entrepreneurs. It's their individual and collective energy that makes the firm viable and distinctive. Typically, it is the employees and not the founders who spend most of their time in the 'front line' with customers and potential customers and who therefore do more to shape the appeal and business formula that the firm exhibits in its early days.

I love entrepreneurial firms. They are creating all the jobs and all the wealth of America, Europe and Asia, while the big established corporations are leeches on the body of the economy. But I don't believe that one man or one woman is always the central force behind a new firm.[3] That just

---

[3] Clearly they sometimes are, easyJet is largely the creation of Stelios Haji-Io-annau, Southwest Airlines of Herb Kelleher, Disney of Walt Disney, furniture group DFS of Graham Kirkham, and so forth. But it's a funny thing. The more you know about a really successful company, from the inside, the less crucial the founders appear. Founders do many great things but they usually also have great flaws and need to be surrounded by many other people who can correct them. Like parents, founders are always necessary but never sufficient. Even someone like Richard Branson, whom most people think of as an archetypical founder, would not have been anywhere near so successful without a large number of his colleagues, mostly friends, who were with him from early days.

doesn't fit with my experience. In the ventures where I've worked and invested, I'm really hard pressed to identify one classic entrepreneur in the lot of them. Rather than talk of the 'entrepreneur' in a particular venture, we should speak of the 'entrepreneurs', or, if you like, the 'collective entrepreneur'.

Entrepreneurship is *people*, plural. It's the first twenty or so employees, not the first one or two or three or four. It's the team. It's the spirit and balance of the team. *There* is the firm's DNA. It doesn't belong to the founder, however big a personality. Often, the more dominant the founder, the bigger the problem, and the more of a handicap the co-founders and employees have to overcome.

Anyone who's worked in a new business knows this. Only the myth of the entrepreneur – so beloved by journalists and academics, who've rarely worked in a new venture – stops us from recognising this obvious truth.

How can new ventures thrive, against the odds? A star business revels in the new niche it creates. But, if the star makes it in the long haul, it is not just the idea for the new category that counts. What's also essential is that somebody translate the idea into intelligent action. Somebody has to win business from sceptical customers. Somebody has to make sure that competitors can't retaliate. Somebody has to deliver the product or service and please the early customers so much that they come back for more. Somebody has to improve the product so that competitors can't catch up. Somebody has to organise the shop. Somebody has to hire great new people and make them understand what the firm is all about, why it is different and better.

Who is 'somebody'? Maybe one or more of the founders. But, more often than not, most of the really valuable work in the early days is done by other employees, the first people through the star venture's door. These are the people who make the business take off. These are the people who make it valuable. And very often they do it *despite* the founder or founders, not because of them. These 'somebodies' are real entrepreneurs, real value creators.

One venture that I've not yet included in my stars, but hope to soon, is Great Little Trading Company, which sells a wide range of exclusively sourced products for the 'toddler-plus' children of well-off mums via catalogues and the Web. Its boss, Jamie Reeve, believes in the many-headed entrepreneur. He's given all 18 employees the same number of options. 'Success will come through collaboration,' Jamie says, 'so I like the idea that I have the same number of options as the office junior.' Jamie is not completely crazy – he has a sizeable shareholding, which he paid for, in addition to his options.

Here's some hard evidence that relying on the many-headed entrepreneur pays huge dividends. The only venture-capital firm in the world that has the same approach as I have (though it may not appreciate my saying so) is Bain Capital, the Boston-based offshoot of Bain & Company, the strategy consulting firm where I was once a partner. Bain Capital and I share three habits:

★ We are very selective about our investments, preferring to build up existing investments and hold them for a long time, rather than sell and move on to pastures new.

★ We take a very active role in working out the strategy of the ventures where we invest, and do not hesitate to give 'guidance' (or more) to our CEOs, and to replace them if necessary.

★ We have very high expectations for the performance of our investments and the price at which we will eventually sell them.

Nearly all Bain Capital's investments are stars. How good are Bain Capital's returns?

Awesome. The best in the industry, anywhere in the world. For the first ten years of its existence, Bain Capital *doubled the value of its investments, on average, every year.* That is what venture capitalists call a 100 per cent 'internal rate of return' – the average amount at which value goes up, compound, each year. A typical venture-capital rate of return is 10–20 per cent, and 30 per cent is reckoned to be very good; 100 per cent is just astounding. To put it in perspective, if you started with $10,000 and doubled it every year, after a decade you would have more than $10 million.

If you are an employee . . .

★ Find a baby star venture to join, one that's just started or still has few employees. Be sure it really is a star, the largest firm in a fast-growing market niche (see Chapters 11 and 12).

★ Become one of the first 20 employees.

★ Try to find a firm that is generous with the right to buy shares in the company or with 'options' that give you shares in the future if you and the firm do well. You are going to create a lot of value. You should be fairly rewarded for that.

★ If there is an opportunity for investment in the star at any time, put as much of your money into it as you possibly can. Actively seek such opportunities.

★ Think like an owner. This is your company. Play a key role in it. Remember – *you can be Somebody.* As soon as you've signed up, you *are* Somebody.

★ Be sure that the venture will be hugely successful, and that you will be, too. It's just a matter of working out how high the stars – you and the business – can go. Be the most ambitious, the most bullish, the most expansive, the most imaginative, the most forward-looking, the most visionary person in the firm. If other people think the firm can be *this* big or *this* valuable, add a zero or two to the end.

★ Work out whether the venture has yet *translated* its formula into action, along the four dimensions necessary:
  ☆ Has the product been made technically accessible for a large number of customers?
  ☆ Have early prospects been made into customers?
  ☆ Have the customers been delighted?

☆ Is the firm a smoothly oiled machine, with a consistent formula, a reliable way of working and excellent results repeated every time at low cost? If not, choose the missing dimension that is most needed, or where you can help the most, and complete the translation (Chapter 13 tells how).

If you are not yet working in a star venture, make it high priority to find one pronto! Why?

★ *Enjoyment.* It's much more fun to work in a fast-expanding, winning team, where you are in on the ground floor.

★ *Personal growth.* Develop on whatever dimensions you want. There will be plenty of need whatever you want to do.

★ *You will be Somebody.* As an early leader of the firm, you will stand out and be able to invest part of your ego in the firm. In a well-established, large firm you might be Nobody. In a firm that started small but became much bigger, where you were one of the first in, you will be Somebody.

★ *You will get promoted much more easily, more certainly and faster.* A firm that's growing fast is quite different from one that's not. A fast-expanding venture is always short of talent. There are more holes than people to fill them. You will want to be stretched and your colleagues will want to stretch you. It won't be a question of waiting for the boss to quit. The question your colleagues will ask is, 'Could *I* possibly do this job?' If the answer is yes, or even maybe, you'll get it.

(I discovered this when I left BCG, a firm growing at perhaps 10 per cent a year, and joined Bain & Company, which was growing at 40–50 per cent. The work was the same. But, whereas at BCG there were plenty in the promotion queue ahead of me, at Bain there was nobody. I was a failure at BCG. I resigned to avoid being fired. At Bain, I was a star, promoted twice within two years – becoming a partner when I'd just turned 30. My performance hadn't changed. I was the same Richard Koch. But the opportunity was much greater.)

★ *Before long, you are likely to be paid better and to get fat bonuses.* Once a star business has reached a certain size, it can hardly avoid making lots of money and throwing off lots of cash. Some of this bounty is bound to make its way to employees – and remember, that's *before* you take account of the effects of promotion. Within 30 months at Bain, I was making three times what I'd made at BCG – which was generous to start with.

★ You might make a lot of money. I don't mean normal pay. I mean through shares and options. Serious money. That depends, of course, on how well you negotiate and how brave you are about buying shares early.

Do you have potential to start a great venture?

Select the statement in each group that you think is most important to start a venture:

Group 1: A – hard work and long hours; B – determination to succeed; C – finding a high-growth market; D – knowing the right people

Group 2: A – the people you work with; B – having the right idea for what the business should be; C – being the leader in your market niche; D – being well organised

Group 3: A – having plenty of cash; B – providing something different and attractive to certain customers; C – building a unique type of firm; D – having a great founder who is an inspired leader and can communicate with everyone

Group 4: A – making decisions by consensus; B – finding a way of pleasing customers while making high profits; C – building a great brand; D – having a clear set of roles and responsibilities for everyone

Group 5: A – watching cash flow like a hawk; B – being the leader in a high-growth niche; C – having great products and being enthusiastic about them; D – ensuring all employees are happy and united

Group 6: A – finding the right job to suit everyone's skills; B – finding a gap in the market and being first to exploit it; C – keeping ahead of competitors; D – having a clear business plan and sticking to it tenaciously

HOW TO SCORE YOUR ANSWERS

For each A, score 3 points. For each B, 5 points. For each C, 4 points. For each D, 0 points.

Add up the total (minimum 0, maximum 30 points).

WHAT YOUR SCORE MEANS

25–30 points: As long as you seriously want to make money as an entrepreneur, you can definitely do so.

18–25 points: You're on the right track; prospects are good. Look at where you chose A or D and read the rest of the book carefully.

10–17 points: Take the test again after reading the book. Starting a great business is still possible, as long as you get the right ideas.

0–9 points: You are probably better suited to being an employee than to being an entrepreneur. But find a job in a star business and you can still do extremely well.

If you are a founder or an aspiring entrepreneur . . .

If you want to start a business, the reasons to aim for a star are even more compelling. You can put just as much skill and effort into a non-star as into a star business. But the results will be totally different. The star business will be *much* easier to build and *much* more rewarding. How do you do this?

★ Find a star idea – Chapters 8–10 guide you here. Or evolve your existing business into a star (for example, by developing any small part of your venture that is or could become a star) – Chapters 7 and 14 will tell you all you need to know.

★ Give as much thought to the selection of your first 20 employees as to starting the venture. Realise how important these people will be.

★ Nurture the many-headed entrepreneur. Give the first 20 employees a generous share of the company.[4] Even if this seems against your interests, it will not be. The pie will be so much bigger – and, if the venture is a star, the pie will be huge. How can the most important

---

[4] I am often asked, 'How much?' There is, of course, no universally applicable formula, but a good rule of thumb is that the top individuals (founders etc.) should get no more than ten times the equity allocated to person number 20. In practice, few founders are willing to be this generous, but those who are never regret it. A team is only fully a team if the status and rewards never exceed a 10:1 ratio. If you cannot stomach this, make the team smaller but preserve the ratio. A smaller top team will, however, cost you.

employees really think like owners, if they are not?

★ If the firm fails to grow rapidly, and it really is a star business, it is because you don't have all the right people. Identify the constraint on growth and hire the best person to sort it out.

★ Be willing to take a back seat. Focus on the one or two activities that you are really great at and enjoy.

Are entrepreneurs born or made?

The truth is, we don't know. There is absolutely no rigorous research available.

We all have our pet theories. Mine, based on observing hundreds of successful and unsuccessful entrepreneurs (but without scientific testing), is that there is a wide range of types of people who start valuable ventures. People who appear to be similar in personality both succeed and fail. Some people fail several times before succeeding. Some have a big hit, but can't do an encore.

If there *is* a personality type that is more likely to succeed, both common sense and observation suggest it is likely to exhibit determination, confidence and self-belief, creativity, unconventional thinking and ability to discern patterns where others just see a random picture. These attributes appear somewhat correlated with some personality types defined by reputable psychologists (for example, those of Meredith Belbin), but there is no strong correlation with any one type.

Other alleged attributes of successful entrepreneurs, such as the willingness to work all the hours God sends, are almost always cited as key success factors. There is not a shred of evidence to support this assertion. It is all 'motherhood and apple pie' and, probably, delusion.

For sure, nearly all successful entrepreneurs stress the importance of hard work. But so do 95 per cent or more of all executives, successful or unsuccessful, entrepreneurs or corporate apparatchiks. There is no evidence that hard work, rather than other common attributes such as determination, vision, egotism and the ability to generate new ideas and believe in them, is the source of success. What is clearly true is that a huge number of unsuccessful entrepreneurs and unsuccessful managers work extremely hard. It's also plain that some wealthy entrepreneurs, such as Donald Trump, Warren Buffett, Richard Branson and now Bill Gates, spend a lot of time doing things other than work (having fun, broadcasting, philanthropy). My own experience is that, as I have made more money and started more successful ventures, the less I have worked. Hard work is either a red herring, or negatively correlated with success.

Look at the issue a different way. What is irrefutable is that most very successful ventures are star businesses, leaders in high-growth niches. Some people may have more intrinsic ability to create star ventures than others, I guess because they are more creative and unconventional, are deeply immersed in a particular activity or know a particular market extremely well and can see the gaps.

What I know is true is that it is possible to teach people (1) the importance of starting a star venture rather than the great majority of ventures that are not stars, (2) how to dream up possible star ideas, (3) how to test them to see if they are likely to work and (4) how to put them into practice. I also know that starting a venture is a team effort, where different types of people all have vital contributions.

I conclude that anyone who truly wants to start a great business, and has determination and self-confidence together with at least average intelligence, has a good chance of doing so – provided they have the knowledge necessary. That knowledge is (a) the template for a successful venture (that is, it must be a star) and (b) the way to set about creating such a venture, described in this book.

If you are or could be an investor . . .

★ Invest only in a star business. Check it really is a star – see Chapters 8 and 12 – before you part with your money.

★ Encourage the founders to take a broad perspective of the many-headed entrepreneur.

★ Have very high expectations and insist on radical change if the expectations are not met – see Chapter 15. If there is no other way to get growth and market share back on track, change the CEO.

Conclusion

If you are going to work for a living, you might as well work as one of the first 20 people in a new star venture. You can be Somebody. It will be the time of your life.

If you want to be a founding entrepreneur, I'll show you how to create your own star venture.

And the best secret of all? It's not as hard as you might think, if you know how. Life, it has been wisely said, is difficult. But making a fortune is much easier! It's time to find out how.

5

The art of
creating stars

*The secret of success is to know something
nobody else knows.*
Aristotle Onassis

When I give a talk about how easy it is to find great stars, there's one question that *always* comes up. 'What you're saying is we should find great ventures,' the objector pipes up, 'but come on, Einstein, that's obvious and doesn't take us very far. It's no use telling us to found a star business without telling us *how* we can spot the stars and avoid the dogs. If it really were that easy, we'd all become millionaires. It just can't be that simple.'

You may be thinking the same thing.

It's a question I love, and the more sceptical the questioner, the better. Although it's an intelligent question, it follows conventional wisdom and betrays a complete lack of understanding of the power of the star idea. My contention, amazing as it sounds, is that *there is a proven way that is likely to lead you to a star business.* That way is described in the chapters that follow, especially Chapters 8, 9 and 10.

First, though, I'd like to explain in this short chapter why striving after a star business is a much better idea than simply saying 'find a great business', why the star approach is not as obvious as it sounds.

The star idea is unusual and specific, and stops you wasting time

If somebody tells you, 'Find a terrific new venture that will become very profitable', that's not a lot of help. It doesn't tell you where or how to look. But, if the advice is 'Find a star business', that's much more helpful and concrete. In fact it excludes the great majority of business ideas. It even excludes the great majority of new ventures that survive and manage to make a living.

Recall what a star business is. It is the *largest company* in its niche. That niche must also *grow fast*, at least 10 per cent a year over the long haul. Both conditions must apply, or it isn't a star.

Most businesses do not lead their niche. Few niches manage 10 per cent growth a year. Only about 5 per cent of surviving businesses, and a much lower proportion of possible new ventures, will satisfy both requirements.

That means you can forget about more than 95 per cent of the ideas you may have. For every 20 ideas you have, you can junk 19 of them, confidently and securely, without doing any more thinking. That saves an awful lot of time. If you had progressed any one of those 19 ideas, and found someone to put up the money to start them, you would have invested years of your life and a lot of somebody else's cash (and perhaps some of your own) in a venture that can never give you a great return. Most likely, it would have gone belly up, sooner or (even worse) later.

The first value of the star idea is that it stops you putting time and effort into ideas that are almost guaranteed to give you a poor return on your sweat. And nearly all ideas, sadly, fall in this category.

This is where the star-business idea scores over the 'terrific-business' idea. You can convince yourself that anything has the potential to be a terrific business. But you can't convince yourself so easily, or, if you are honest, easily at all, that your idea will be among the 5 per cent or fewer businesses that are correctly defined as stars. The definition of a star venture is not subjective. It is objective, and requires two very difficult conditions to be met.

You have to state *why and how* your business is going to be the leader. If the niche already exists, so too does a leader. Displacing an incumbent leader is always possible, but it is difficult. It's not something to bet on, unless you have a source of competitive advantage that is totally compelling.

Typically, star-venture start-ups create their own niche. If the niche proves viable, the venture starts in the wonderful position of 'born leader'.

To create a viable new niche is tough. The large majority of attempts to create a niche fail. Why? Two conditions must be met:

★ **There must be a gap in the market.** All existing players must have overlooked the gap, or judged it too small, too unprofitable or too implausible. For sure, this is possible. But it is not very likely.

★ **There must be a market in the gap.** The gap must be large enough to support at least one new venture (yours) profitably. This, too, is not probable.

If you follow the star theory, you not only have to argue that the niche will be created and that your new venture will remain the leader in it. You also have to believe that the niche will grow consistently at 10 per cent – and preferably much more – each year. The bar is high. If you think your niche will vault it, you must have good reasons. Of course, nobody can know what the growth rate of an as-yet-uncreated market will be. But just asking the question will throw a lot of doubt on all but the most robust of propositions.

Star ventures are rare. The requirements are onerous. Why, then, do I say that thinking up a great new star business is possible? Because you have a huge head start if you know precisely what you are looking for, and can reject, easily and quickly, the great majority of ideas you and your friends may have.

Let me tell you a secret. Most 'brilliant' managers and 'superstar' entrepreneurs perform miracles not because of their brilliance, but because they are in the right place at the right time. Almost anyone reasonably competent, sitting where they sat, could have done pretty much the same. And, when successful firms start to fail, the same is nearly always true in reverse. Even the world's best executive stands a poor chance of reversing the capricious momentum of markets and rivals when they have it in for a firm.

As Professor Phil Rosenzweig of the IMD business school in Switzerland demonstrates, nearly all the usual explanations of business success are useless and exaggerate the impact that individual managers have.[5] When a company is doing well, we explain its success in terms of its leadership and culture. When the company starts to do badly, we make opposite attributions – we find all kinds of reasons why the leader and the culture have screwed up. In reality, we are not explaining success or failure: we are just rationalising it.

Though it goes against everything we like to believe, everything we read in papers and books, the curious truth is that executives have much less influence than they and we like to believe, once a firm's positioning is set. One executive versus another is almost completely irrelevant, unless he or she makes a brave and dangerous decision to try to transform a firm's positioning. This is rare. Even when the attempt is made, it fails more often than it succeeds.

The one time when individuals can dependably make a difference and put themselves in a great position is:

★ when they select the positioning for a new or young venture;

★ when they realise that success comes from creating a star firm (this is the only general and reliable reason for business success, since nearly all stars are very successful,

---

5 Phil Rosenzweig (2007), *The Halo Effect . . . and the Eight Other Business Delusions That Deceive Managers* (New York: Free Press).

so long as they stay stars – and, crucially, the other way round: nearly all very successful firms are stars); and

★ when they determine to start a star venture.

Here's an even better reason for optimism: there is a proven route to creating new star ventures. I know. I've travelled this road several times. Although I haven't always been successful when I set out to create a star venture, I succeeded more times than I failed.

And, since my travels, I've worked out how to make the odds of success even more favourable. I've codified what works and what doesn't. I've reflected on why things worked and why they didn't. That's what this book is all about. In your hands you hold the first, and so far the only, guide to starting a star business.

OK, that's it. I've cleared my throat. I've tried to answer the doubters. If you're with me so far, you're about to find out how you too can find a star business.

6

Born stars

Some are born great, some achieve greatness, and some have greatness thrust upon 'em.
William Shakespeare

Two of my five stars were indisputably *born* stars. They created a new niche that they led from the start.

Belgo: the monastery-restaurant chain

How different can a restaurant be from all other restaurants? Imagine going through a long dark tunnel and emerging in an underground cavern. A dozen monks are fluttering around in long gowns, rushing between long wooden tables where people sit, not in twos and fours but in large groups. The people are drinking beer from obscure monasteries in Belgium, eating mussels from huge steaming pots, the kind that belong on ovens and not tables. You see massive plates of fries served with mayonnaise, no tomato ketchup in sight. You hear a huge racket, a din of voices amplified by the stone surroundings.

Welcome to the first Belgo restaurant, opened in 1992

near Camden Lock in London. Welcome to an overnight sensation, with customers lining up round the block to get in. Welcome to the only venture I've ever known where it was clear after the first week that it was a star business where the sky was the limit.

This was a business that two unusual guys had tried, and failed, to get off the ground for several years. True, they looked an odd couple. On the left was André Plisnier, a tall, rather gloomy individual in his late thirties who was half-Belgian but who spoke with an engaging upper-class English accent, a kind of miscast Hercule Poirot. He had been a restaurant manager. On the right towered Denis Blais, a maverick, French Canadian, twenty-something ex-bartender dressed entirely in black and looking more movie star than entrepreneur. They tried to interest me in their bizarre ideas for a themed restaurant. In fact they had six theme ideas, each one for a different national cuisine and each one with a set of theatrical and design ideas to match the food.

We fell into discussing their proposal. 'It's great to be different,' I said, 'and the idea with the waiters dressed as monks serving Belgian beer and food is the most distinctive of your ideas. How can you be sure that the demand will be there? Is anybody doing that already?'

'Nobody in England,' André said. 'But there is a chain of Belgian restaurants in Paris called Leon and they are always full. We've taken some of their ideas but we've added our own. By dressing the waiters as monks we can make the connection between Belgium and monastery beer inescapable.'

'And by making the restaurant a huge open room with

nothing but wooden benches and stone walls we can make it seem like a monastery hall,' Denis added. 'It will look like no other restaurant in town. We are paying particular attention to all the design details.'

'I can see that from the budget you've submitted,' I said. 'To ask for three hundred and fifty thousand pounds to start a single small restaurant is ridiculous. Why can't you cut down on the expense of the fixtures and fittings?'

'We want the place to be really authentic and also glitzy,' Denis responded. 'We want our customers to feel that they are getting a forty-pound meal for twenty pounds. There will be nowhere else where they can get such an unusual experience and excellent service for the same price.'

'I'm glad you mentioned that,' I said. 'If we have such high fixed costs, and also spend so much money on having lots of waiters, how are we going to make money?'

'We've thought of that,' said André. 'The menu is very carefully selected. We are aiming for very high gross margins, around 73 per cent. We can do that because we're serving Belgian peasant food at quite high prices. People think mussels are expensive, but they're not. We can sell a kilogram pot of mussels with a great sauce and *frites* for £10, and it costs us less than £2.50. *Frites* are just about the highest-margin food there is, and most dishes will come with *frites* or have them ordered on the side. Our Belgian monastery beers are quite expensive, and there is no direct comparison the customers can make, as we'll be the only suppliers in England. And the convivial atmosphere and noise of the dining hall will encourage people to drink a lot of beer.'

'I'm the person who will be in charge of food production,'

Denis chimed in. 'I'm planning it like a fast-food factory. The food order will be transmitted direct from waiters' consoles to the kitchen and the food will always be cooked within ten minutes and delivered right away. My ideal is very high-quality food but cooked in exactly the same way and the same time, like an upmarket McDonald's.'

'And we plan to get customers in and out as quickly as possible,' said André. 'We will take the drinks order as soon as we seat anyone. At the end we will provide the bill and accept payment within two minutes. We plan to get people in and out within 45 minutes or an hour at the outside.'

'That's great,' I shot back, 'as that's the only way the numbers will stack up. Because you propose to spend so much on the restaurant itself, we'll only get our money back if there's very high volume of customers. So I like the idea of a quality fast restaurant. I reckon we need three or four sittings a day at each table in order to make enough money. But there's a flaw in your reasoning. It's one thing for us to serve the customers promptly, but what happens if they just hang around at the end of the meal?'

'We won't let them,' answered Denis. 'When they book, we'll tell them that they have a slot, just like an aeroplane waiting to take off. If they book for seven, they'll need to be out by eight thirty. We'll tell them when they book and when they arrive that we'll want the table back at such-and-such time.'

'Do you think we can get away with that?'

'Only if we're hot. But we plan to be hot.'

'What about the name?' I asked. 'All the branding experts say the name matters a lot. The name must associate the venture with the experience.'

'We want to call it Belgo, pronounced Bell-go,' they replied in unison. 'We'll be the first in our own category of Belgian monastery restaurants and Belgo will instantly recall the idea. There will only be one place to go for that experience and Belgo is its name.'

'You're very keen on this concept,' I concluded, 'and you've got some great answers to my questions. But I understand you've been planning this for years. Why haven't you done this already?'

'Nobody will back us with the money.'

I wasn't sure it would work. In fact I reckoned Belgo had at best a 50–50 chance of success. Would it really be a star business? Would it create its own category? Would the niche grow rapidly? I reckoned the idea was sufficiently outlandish and distinctive that, if it took off, Belgo would be able to stay the leader in its niche for a long time. The key question was whether the customers would come. If they did, it would be a star business.

The great thing about any branded retail venture – a restaurant, a shop, a bar – is that, *if* the first one works, the second one will, and the third, and so on. Roll-out can ensure rapid growth. If the formula is high-margin and gives high return on capital, you can make a small fortune from a small investment, funding future growth out of the cash flow from the first outlet or outlets.

So I told the boys that I would invest. After so many let-downs, they couldn't believe it. They went off to a bar to celebrate, with smiles a mile wide.

The customers came. Belgo started to throw off cash like crazy. When we had just two restaurants, we sold the business to a consortium led by Luke Johnson, a well-known British entrepreneur, who then took it public. My investment of £300,000 turned into £6 million. André and Denis got an even better return.

Betfair: the $2 billion star

You'll recall Andrew (Bert) Black from the Introduction. As a keen punter, Bert wanted plant a bomb under the enemy – the big bookmaking firms. His idea for revolutionising the betting market worldwide was to build a 'betting exchange', a Web-based system for matching opposing bets from individuals.

By the time I came across Betfair early in 2001, it had been going a few months. To the untutored eye it looked a disaster zone – a bizarre idea never tried before; young, untested, inexperienced executives; trifling revenues; large losses; undercapitalised and cash reserves almost exhausted. And Andrew Black, with his penchant for wearing shorts in the office even in the depths of winter, resembled the classic mad inventor.

Yet as soon as I heard about Betfair and spoke to the founders I knew it was for me, because it was the clearest example I'd seen for ages of a star business that – mishaps aside – was likely to become very large and valuable. Minuscule and apparently weak as it was, Betfair was already the leader in a very fast-growth niche, one I guessed could become enormous.

The betting market was huge, but it was not high-growth. Yet Betfair was different. By offering a different kind of deal for punters, Betfair was creating its own market, the 'betting exchange' market. Traditional book-makers were not in that market – they could not provide a betting exchange. So, the way I look at it, Betfair did not have a tiny share of a huge market. It had a very large share – there was a smaller exchange, started the same year – of a tiny market. And that market, tiny as it was, was growing very fast. In fact, Betfair was growing at more than 30 per cent every *month*. That is incredibly fast, more than doubling every three months.

Though nobody was paying attention to Betfair at the time, and it was almost bankrupt, it was a star business. I was able to buy a good chunk of it for a knockdown price. What did I know that all other money people didn't? Nothing. Except that it was a star business.

When they buy businesses, all venture capitalists look hard at the technology, the management, the market. They get into all sorts of complex investigation. They hire consultants to assess the technology and the market, accountants to crawl over the books, and lawyers to tie the managers in knots and do whatever lawyers do. I did none of those things. I knew Betfair was a star business. That was enough for me.

All right, as a gambler I liked the idea of Betfair, because it offered better odds than the bookmakers and, if it was successful, it would be a thorn in their side. Every punter loves to hate the bookies. But, then again, I am not a follower of Victor Kiam, who famously bought Remington because he liked shaving with its razor. I never buy into a company because I like its product. For the first couple of years that I was a part-owner and director of Betfair, I didn't register as a user. To be honest, I'm not very good with technology and I didn't know how to go online and bet. I remember being ridiculed by some of my fellow Betfair directors when I remarked, nearly three years after making my investment, that I had just started using the site and found it impressive. How could anyone invest in their baby without giving it an extensive road-test first, without understanding how to use it?

Wilful ignorance is one of my best investment tools. I don't want to know too much before making an investment. I don't want to cloud my judgement, or make the decision difficult. I don't want to know about all the risks or understand them. I just want to be reasonably sure that it's a star business.

That makes life simple and fun. And profitable.

Roll the story forward to today. On 3 April 2006, 23 per cent of Betfair was sold to Softbank of Japan in a deal valuing the firm at £1.54 *billion*. The first half-million pounds' worth of shares I had bought turned into £26.4 million in cash, and my total holding became worth £113 million. The stakes of Bert Black and his co-founder became worth more than £200 million each. Since then Betfair has continued to grow fast. Although we don't really know the new value of Betfair, because it is not quoted on the stock exchange, it is probably (touch wood) much more than Softbank paid. Because we sold fewer than a quarter of our shares, Bert and I certainly hope we continue to sit on a fast-appreciating asset!

7

Stardom thrust upon them

Only learn to seize good fortune, for it is always there.
Johann Wolfgang von Goethe

My remaining three stars were not born that way. They *became* stars. They either 'achieved stardom' or 'had stardom thrust upon them'.

Filofax: twice a star

Around 1910, G. F. Parker, a Canadian engineer, created the personal-organiser niche, setting up Lefax Inc. in Philadelphia.[6] Before Lefax there were diaries, address books and 'day books' or journals for jotting down notes. Parker created a new category: a six-ring, loose-leaf binder

---

[6] This section draws heavily on an unpublished work by David Collischon, the creator of the modern Filofax system: David Collischon (2007), *No Flash in the Pan: The Story of Filofax 1975 to 1990*. David has been most generous with his time and unique knowledge in answering many questions about the early days of the business. The interpretation of Filofax's history here, though, is very much my own, as are any errors that may have survived.

system for professional data. His idea was to publish scientific, technical, medical and other data sheets in loose-leaf format, including week-on-a-page diaries. He introduced some 5,000 different sheets but could not keep them up to date, so he provided blank data sheets for users to enter their own information. Parker soon had a successful star business on his hands.

It was while in the US that a British army officer named Colonel Disney saw and admired the Lefax system. He had some friends with a printing business in England and persuaded them to start manufacturing Lefax products under licence. The new business, Norman & Hill Limited, opened its doors in 1921. Grace Scurr, originally a temporary secretary who, like Disney, became fascinated by the personal-organiser system, soon came to run Norman & Hill, the forerunner of Filofax.

The organiser system gained a strong following with the clergy and army officers. Mobile professions such as doctors, architects and salesmen also became dedicated users. The business was starved of capital and grew only slowly – it was a tiny cash cow rather than a star. In 1928 Grace dreamed up Filofax as a trademark, though initially only for stationery (the loose-leaf sheets sold to go in the organisers).

By 1975, Norman & Hill had turnover of only £22,600. Then David Collischon, a mid-level publishing executive, came on the scene. He had been a user of the N&H system since 1959 and thought it was a great concept, but totally underexploited. In 1975 he started Pocketfax as a mail-order business selling Filofax products. For the first time, he provided a 'ready-made' organiser (previously users had to buy the wallets and whatever selection of papers they wanted separately), comprising a slim wallet, a diary, a Tube (subway) map, some plain leaves in various colours, cash leaves, a credit-card holder (a Collischon innovation) and a flyleaf.

Within four years, David's star venture, started with only £500 capital, had sales nearly double those that N&H achieved in 1975, and had taken 54 years to reach. He used the profits from Pocketfax to buy Norman & Hill in 1980 for £9,000.

David changed the concept of the product from stationery to fashion accessory. As he told me, 'In 1980, Letts diaries sold for £1.50. We sold at £25. Impossible to sell the two side by side – after all, Filofax was then viewed as just another diary, selling mainly in old-fashioned stationers' stores. But my idea was to introduce Filofax to top-end, fashion-related and fashionable stores, and greatly increase the number of retail outlets. Selling Filofax beside leather handbags retailing for £100-plus, it looked cheap. Before long we were selling in Harrods, Liberty, Browns, Harvey Nichols, Fortnum & Mason, Paul Smith, Selfridges, and John Lewis, all upscale retailers. Having created this exclusivity and demand in the fashion stores and the press, we were later able to sell the same product through mass-market retailers without damaging the top end.'

Paul Smith, the fashion designer, played an important role in the growth of Filofax. Like David, he had been a Filofax user and about the same time David started Pocketfax he began to display Filofax prominently in his store in London's Covent Garden. (Everything in the store was black or white. A black Filofax was displayed in the window, with an open Mont Blanc pen perched on top.) In the late seventies and early eighties, Paul's business took off internationally. At fashion trade fairs across Europe, he exhibited Filofax products alongside his own.

Paul's push was important in getting Filofax into the fashion-accessory trade in Continental Europe, Japan and California. Filofax developed an international network of agents; those in France, Germany, Belgium, Switzerland, Holland, Italy and Australia all came from the garment trade. Success in prestige outlets outside the UK was important in getting Filofax into some of its upscale British accounts. These in turn helped to get the brand into prestigious American outlets in the US such as Saks, Bloomingdale's and Neiman Marcus.

Almost everywhere, Filofax became one of the aspirational products of the 1980s, and a wonderfully profitable star business. From 1975 to 1987, when it floated, sales multiplied 589 times, with growth over 40 per cent a year. David's original £500 turned into a paper value of £17.2 million, an increase of more than 34,000 times. A year after floating, Filofax's value had more than doubled again. Filofax became the leading supplier of personal organisers – a fast-growth niche – everywhere in the world outside the US. The only problem was keeping up with demand.

Then came the fall, and my opportunity. From 1988, Filofax sales dipped and the company went from stellar profits to mounting losses. By 1990 it was bleeding £2 million a year. When I asked to see him, David Collischon told me the problem was 'the death of the yuppie' following the stock market crash in 1987. My probing in the market revealed a different explanation. Filofax had lost market share and its star status was in jeopardy. Personal organisers were still a high-growth market, but in its home market Filofax had lost out to Microfile, a small firm peddling lookalike organisers through mass-market outlets at less than half Filofax's price. In the UK, Microfile was taking away Filofax's star status, having become nearly as big as Filofax by value and much larger by number of organisers sold.

Could Filofax be turned around and recover its clear star position in personal organisers? Sitting in a deckchair on a roof in Brighton, I realised that it could.

Microfile was profitable, making about 10 per cent return on sales. Microfile was selling organisers at half Filofax's price. Filofax was losing market share because it appeared ridiculously expensive, at least in the mainstream retail outlets that now comprised the bulk of the personal-organiser market. Yet the shopkeepers I talked to said they thought Filofax deserved a small brand premium, perhaps 15 per cent more than Microfile.

Therefore, I reasoned, Filofax had a massive cost problem, which was also an opportunity. If Microfile could sell organisers at half the Filofax price, and make money, then Filofax could, too. If Filofax could get the same costs as Microfile, and sold its organisers at 15 per cent (instead of 100 per cent) more than its rival's price, then Filofax could recover market share and make more than 25 per cent return on sales (the 10 per cent made by Microfile plus the 15 per cent price premium). Filofax would then be a star business again, and very valuable.

In 1990, nobody wanted to buy Filofax or invest in it. Everyone else saw a sinking ship, a fad that was past its time, a firm about to go bust. I saw a star business that could make a lot of money again. I believed in the star concept. I didn't know how to revive Filofax. I just knew that it was possible. We organised a rights issue and began buying shares when they were on the floor. David Collischon co-operated fully, agreeing to sell a large part of his stake and step aside from his executive role, while remaining non-executive chairman.

Again, I violated venture-capital rules, bringing in as new CEO a friend and former LEK consultant, Robin Field, who had no experience in Filofax's industry (we look at LEK Consulting below). His mission, I said, was to make Filofax a star again and slash costs. Apart from that, I told him, I had no idea what to do. Robin found that the product line had expanded beyond all control.

'The same basic binder,' he said, 'was available in a bewildering variety of sizes and huge assortment of – mainly exotic – skins. I don't know what a karung is, but I inherited an awful lot of its skin in 1990. Similarly, name a subject – bridge, chess, photography, bird watching, windsurfing, whatever. Filofax had commissioned specialist inserts, had tens of thousands printed, and put them into the warehouse. The result, of course, was not only a huge overhang of worthless stock, not only an administrative burden of vast complexity, but also total confusion among our retailers.'

Robin reduced headcount from 200 to 75, slashed the product range and introduced a complete new range of much cheaper Filofaxes. Within a year, 85 per cent of organisers sold were new models, Filofax had gone past Microfile to recover its clear star status and the firm was highly profitable and cash-positive. We sold Filofax in 1998 for seven times the rights-issue price.

Filofax is interesting because it was made a star twice – by David Collischon and later by Robin Field and me. David took a minuscule cash cow and made it a mighty star. In the late 1980s, Filofax lost market share at such a fast rate that its sales plummeted while the personal-organiser category was still growing at more than 10 per cent a year. The firm was well on the way to becoming a question mark – and probably a dead one – before it was turned around. There are three insights lurking here.

★ **A cash cow can be turned into a star** when the *concept of the product category is transformed* – David's vision of personal organisers as upscale fashion accessories re-invented the whole market.

★ **Product concepts evolve.** The idea of personal organisers as expensive fashion accessories lasted less than a decade. Competition cannot be ignored, especially when it changes the product concept. Because personal organisers similar to Filofax could be made much more cheaply by competitors, a mass market developed that ultimately subverted the idea of the personal organiser as fashion accessory. When competitors sold something similar at half the price, Filofax sales collapsed. The only route back to profitable stardom was to accept the new definition of the product category and beat rivals at their own game. Robin and I never really understood David's vision of Filofax as being unique. We accepted personal organisers as a mass-market stationery product intended to be useful rather than decorative. If we had shared David's vision we could never have turned Filofax around. We focused on recovering market leadership in the market as it was, as defined by competitors.

★ **A star that is fast losing market share, or an ex-star that has lost it, may be an attractive prospect**. Nobody wants a star that is plunging to earth or already on the floor. With the right strategy, however, ex-stars can sometimes recover their greatness. They may come dirt cheap. A good source of stars is ex-stars.

Plymouth Gin: how to 'achieve stardom'

Plymouth Gin is England's oldest gin distiller. The distillery is located within a former Dominican monastery built around 1431, and it's been operating since 1793. If you looked through a bottle of our Plymouth Gin, you could see a monk on the inside of the back label. The front label depicted the *Mayflower*. On 16 September 1620, the Pilgrims set out for America on the *Mayflower*, having stayed for two weeks in the former monastery, by then Plymouth's town meeting house.

Plymouth Gin was once a star. Plymouth Gin can be made only in Plymouth, whereas London Gin can be made anywhere. As the only distiller in Plymouth, the brand effectively enjoyed a monopoly, reinforced by its distinctive fruity taste through the use of 'botanicals' as flavouring. Up to the 1920s, Plymouth was the largest English premium gin and generally acknowledged among connoisseurs as the finest.

By 1996, however, Plymouth Gin was almost defunct. It had deliberately been run down by its owner, Allied Domecq, to avoid competition with Beefeater, the leading premium gin owned by Allied.

Two partners and I acquired the Plymouth distillery and brand and set about revitalising it on a shoestring, with a total investment around £1.5 million. Our thesis was that the premium-gin market was again growing at around 10 per cent a year and that Plymouth Gin, with its rich brand heritage and unique taste, could recover its leadership position, at least in the UK.

We were attracted to the gin market because nobody else was. The vodka sector was undergoing a huge renaissance with masses of new entrants and innovation. In the late 1990s there were about 100 major product launches of new vodkas or vodka variants, each backed by multi-million-dollar investment. The neglect of gin, which was a massive market, made a bargain-basement purchase attractive to us, provided we could generate some excitement. Plymouth would give us a unique property and a ready exit at a high price, if we managed to recover some niche leadership for Plymouth. There were only four premium-gin brands in the world – Gordon's, Beefeater, Tanqueray and Bombay Sapphire – and, with the exception of the last, they were all, we felt, a bit boring.

At first we made little headway. We couldn't afford advertising. We encouraged the new management to use public relations as a way of getting the brand noticed again. But sales budgets were not met and we had to let two CEOs go in rapid succession. One of my partners was John Murphy, formerly the chairman of Interbrand, a highly regarded consumer-brand consultancy. Even in our darkest hours, John, who became non-executive chairman of Plymouth, was adamant that the brand could recover its leading position in premium gin. I clung to my star-venture mantra: that this had been a star business before and could become one again. Still, the numbers were not good. Sales in our first year were a disastrous, negligible 4,500 cases. Our capital shrank to just £150,000, and the three partners had to provide personal guarantees to keep Plymouth going.

Our breakthrough came when we hired a new CEO, Charles Rolls, who was a good friend of a friend of mine. In choosing Charles, we broke four cardinal venture-capital rules. We hired someone with no drinks industry experience, someone who had never been a CEO before, someone who was from our social circle and someone who was an ex-consultant (with Bain & Company). We hired Charles because we knew he understood strategy, because we thought he would be excellent at PR and because of his determination to make Plymouth Gin a star again. We made Charles an equal partner with the three of us.

It was third CEO lucky. Together with John Murphy, Charles gained massive free publicity for the brand, and sales, though still low, began to climb. We knew that, to generate a buzz and recover leadership, we needed to differentiate the brand from other premium gins. We used the brand's rich history to portray it as quirky, and dug up obscure facts about its heritage to feed to journalists. For all our talk of quality and authenticity, however, we lacked any tangible product differentiation. Only one supermarket chain – and a downmarket one at that (Asda) – would list our gin.

After many talks with Sean Harrison, Plymouth's head distiller, Charles became convinced that we could differentiate Plymouth by increasing its alcoholic strength. As Sean explained, it is the essential oils in a gin that generate its smell and taste. The oils are held in the liquid by alcohol. Higher-proof gins have more taste. Well-travelled, sophisticated gin drinkers appreciated the difference between high-strength duty-free gin and ordinary gin of the same brand. The only problem with raising alcoholic strength – and a huge one – was the cost in duty. Recently, Gordon's had gone the other way with its gin, cutting from 40 per cent to 37.5 per cent alcohol, making massive extra profit as a result.

Charles found some old papers in the distillery attic dating from the early 1900s, showing that Plymouth was then 45.2 per cent alcohol. To go back to that strength would be prohibitively expensive. Somehow, Charles invented the number 41.2 per cent. If we put Plymouth up from 40 to 41.2 per cent, the taste would improve and we would be higher in alcohol than our three main competitors.[7] We decided to make a huge song and dance about our higher alcohol content. We called it the 'Victorian strength', harking back to great days for Britain and Plymouth Gin. Charles and John redesigned the bottle to make it similar to a Victorian one, put a cork in the top, and promoted the idea that when the monk's feet were getting dry it was time to buy another bottle of Plymouth.

---

[7] Tanqueray had bravely kept its gin at 47 per cent alcohol, despite the massive extra duty it had to pay. But this made Tanqueray far too expensive, at least in the UK with its high duty, and they sold virtually nothing there. Tanqueray also made little effort to promote the benefits of its higher strength.

The strategy began to work. Then we had a stroke of fortune — it's impossible to say to what extent it was because of our new strategy, or just pure luck. One afternoon in 1997 we had a call from BBC TV telling us to watch the *Food and Drink* programme that evening. We saw Jilly Goulden announce to her 5 million viewers the result of a survey of independent gin tasters. She declared Plymouth Gin the best on the market. She also rubbished Gordon's for quietly dropping its strength.

The response was instantaneous. Within days we were into all main UK supermarkets. Over four years our sales rose 17 times and Plymouth became the leader in the premium retail market. To internationalise the brand, we sold half of it in 2000 to Vin & Sprit, owners of Absolut Vodka, at a total valuation approaching £30 million. V&S relaunched Plymouth Gin throughout the world, especially in America. I sold my remaining shares in 2002, making 12 times my money.

Three aspects of this story stand out.

1. **PR is only as good as the reality behind it.** To recover leadership requires real differentiation and added value for the consumer. It's pointless to *claim* you are better: you have to *prove* that you are different, and the difference has to appeal. It took us a while to realise this. Any longer and we would have gone bust.

2. **It's not as unusual as you might expect to find a hole in the market** — even a market as big and profitable as gin. Seek a hole and sooner or later you will find one. John Murphy went on to exploit another market gap,

this time in beer. Britain has the fourth-largest brewing industry in the world, and it also has some very different beers – ales, porters, stouts and fruit beers – with great appeal worldwide. Yet until recently British brewers exported very little. John set up St Peter's Brewery as an international brand of British beer. His new star venture has clocked up growth of 40 per cent a year. Another curious hole that shouldn't have existed, but did.

Charles Rolls also found another hole after Plymouth Gin, again based on superior taste. His new star venture, Fever-Tree, created a niche in the huge but dull 'mixers' soft-drink market, dominated around the world by Schweppes. Fever-Tree provides the finest possible, all-natural ingredients, so its mixers complement premium and super-premium drinks. Despite significantly higher prices, Fever-Tree has already proved that serious spirits drinkers will pay a premium for great mixers. The extra cost is a small proportion of the drink's total, and makes a real difference to the taste.

3. **Timing is everything.** We were the first 'new' brand to challenge the existing leaders and make the gin strength our key selling point. A few years later, many new gin brands came on the market, nearly all with some strange and quite high new alcohol percentage. Once everyone is playing the same game, the advantage disappears. To stand a good chance of creating a star you must not only be the first in the niche you create, but also the first with your key consumer benefit.

LEK Consulting: imitation precludes uniqueness

Although I invested in Betfair in spring 2001, shortly after it started, I had nothing to do with its creation. I was generally reckoned to be a founder of LEK, back in 1983, even though I actually joined three months after its predecessor firm, Lawrence and Evans, had opened its doors. I seem to make a habit of arriving at the party a few months after it starts. But what a party we had at LEK!

For me it lasted six years and they were without doubt the time of my life. Not always the happiest time. Certainly not the easiest or most stress-free. But without question the time I grew up the most, developed the most, made the most intense professional friendships, and learned the most. And made a few millions, which have been cloning subsequently.

LEK was easy to start, and it may well be the way you start, or have already started, as an entrepreneur – by doing what you did before, but in your own new venture. Jim Lawrence, Iain Evans and I were consultants in our early thirties. We worked in a peculiar but very lucrative and fast-growth branch called 'strategy consulting'. Basically this means telling the heads of Fortune 500 firms where to focus their efforts – stock answer, on their stars – and how to outrun their rivals. We knew how to operate this business, and run very large teams of young eager beavers who were MBAs (masters of business administration) or young graduates from the world's top universities. We knew how to sell to CEOs.

We were so confident that we were good at strategy

consulting, that, perhaps rather naively, we saw no reason why we couldn't do what we were doing for ourselves, rather than for the benefit of our senior partners.

The way we became entrepreneurs was classic. A good half of new ventures start the same way. Someone is good at being a cab driver, being a physician, baking cakes, being a chef, tending a bar, inventing the transistor, running a PR firm, buying and selling bonds. Whatever. Instead of doing it for somebody else, they do it for themselves.

This 'easy' route to a new venture also leads to rude awakenings. If you start a new business with a totally new formula, you tend to be humble and unsurprised when you encounter choppy waters. If you start a business doing what you did before, and the previous business made a lot of money, you expect to do so too.

You are usually wrong. You run up against one of the most basic and unwelcome laws of strategy. To succeed, a venture has to do something different. It has to be a leader. And to be *really* successful you have to be a star business – not just number one in a niche, but first in a fast-growth niche.

At LEK, we fell foul of this immutable law of strategy.

Our ace in the hole, we believed, was the unique business formula we knew: the Bain & Company formula. Bill Bain believed that his consultants could have more effect if they worked in a long-term relationship with a small number of clients. The terms of engagement set at the start of the relationship were quite different from the relationship between any other consulting firm and its clients. The pitch made by the partner selling the relationship would go something like this.

'If we decide to work with you,' the partner would tell the CEO of the prospective client, 'we will undertake not to work for any of your competitors. This means that we will be devoted to making you the most successful firm in your industry. Any secrets that you tell us will remain safe with us for ever. In return for our not working with your competitors, we expect *you* not to work with any of *our* competitors. We also expect you not to impose any arbitrary limit on the amount of work we do. If we propose new consulting projects that have a high return on investment, we expect you to agree to those projects, unless you disagree with our assessment of the benefits your company will get from our work.'

As you can imagine, this was a difficult pitch. Yet the Bain approach worked for many clients, especially when a new CEO had been appointed from outside. Bain and the CEO formed a bond designed to raise dramatically the performance of the CEO's organisation. CEOs usually bought Bain's services on the recommendation of other CEO clients of Bain. Bain tended to work for very ambitious CEOs who had been appointed to fat and happy firms, where there was plenty of scope for performance improvement by selling non-core divisions and cutting costs throughout the firm.

The magic of the formula for Bain & Company was that it gained an exclusive charter for consulting within each client. Not only that, but Bain could expand the number of consultants and the billings to each client over time, thus gaining inbuilt growth within each client firm. Each client became a separate niche market, which could grow speedily to high levels. Each client became a star venture for Bain, and a star of the best type – a high-growth monopoly that was extremely profitable and cash-positive.

We wanted LEK to be like Bain. We planned to take one existing client, where we had a warm relationship with the CEO, with us from Bain to LEK. That would provide us with an instant base load of highly profitable work. Then we would simply carry on providing an 'alternative Bain' service, particularly for corporations where Bain worked for a competitor of the corporation, and therefore could not compete with us at LEK.

There was one problem. Bain & Company did not see it our way. They didn't want to lose any of their clients, even when the client CEO wanted to go with us. Most of all, they didn't want to allow any of their partners to defect. Bain slapped a massive lawsuit on our fledgling firm, stopping us gaining the client we wanted, depriving us of revenue, causing us huge legal expenses which were a drop in the ocean to Bain but potentially crippling for us. Worst of all, they tied us up defending the lawsuit when we needed to be out selling work.

We were depressed and distracted by the litigation. It seemed the worst thing that could have happened to us. But in fact it was the best. We owe Bain a huge thank-you for suing us. They forced us to search for our own unique formula. If you have set up a business or are thinking about doing so, this is perhaps the most important lesson for you, too.

Ecologists know that two species of animal that try to exist in exactly the same way become deadly enemies. If two species compete head-on for food, only one of them can win. The other species must change either the food it seeks or the way it hunts for it. If it does neither, the weaker species will die out.

It is the same with business, except the time to extinction is compressed. Any business that imitates another slavishly will not be successful. The numbers are against it. It will be competing in the same market as the market leader. It will be smaller. It will have less appeal to customers. It will be less profitable and usually loss-making. It will have to do something different, or die.

If our plan had succeeded, LEK would have ended up as a smaller, pale imitation of Bain & Company; we could never have had a star business. Happily, we failed to make the formula stick. Later, through having too many young and inexperienced research associates, we stumbled across selling 'competitor analysis' and 'relative cost position' products.

Let us eavesdrop on a chat I had with a close colleague, nearly three years after the birth of LEK, over dinner at my house in Bayswater.

'You must be pleased,' he said, 'with how things are going.'

'Well,' I said, 'we've sold a lot of profitable business, but I keep wondering how long it'll last. We're supposed to be strategy consultants, but we don't have a good strategy for our own firm.'

'Who cares? We'll always think of something to sell, and this cost–position stuff is selling like hot cakes. If that doesn't last, we'll think of something else.'

'But what would we tell a client who was in our position? We'd say that they needed a coherent position, a niche in the market based on a particular type of customer, where they are best at serving the client, with certain clearly defined products. We'd tell them to find a fast-growth market they could dominate. We'd say if they couldn't get a star position, they wouldn't be able to grow profitably in the future.'

We went round in circles for a while, then moved on to talk about personalities. I never did work out what LEK's strategy should be.

Then disaster struck. I think we had six or seven clients at the time, and within a few months four of them were attacked by hostile takeover bids. By this time we had a lot of mouths to feed. We knew that any client that was taken over would become an ex-client. We were seriously worried.

Then it dawned on us that we could use our capability in competitor analysis to help defend our clients. In those days most of the bids were not hard cash, but shares in the bidder. What if we turned our analysis of competitors on to the bidders? Surely we could find some weaknesses in their armoury. Perhaps we could persuade our clients' shareholders to spurn shares in the bidder.

Our biggest client was the Imperial Group, under siege from Hanson. Imperial was a rather fat and happy British conglomerate, with interests in cigarettes, food, drinks, hotels and restaurants. Hanson was a lean-and-mean acquisition machine and a darling of the stock market, using its highly rated shares to take over companies, cut costs and generate cash for ever more ambitious bids. Hanson offered Imperial shareholders a big premium over the previous share price, yet could still show that the acquisition would increase Hanson's earnings per share. Imperial's case looked hopeless.

My partner Iain Evans then turned the full force of LEK's competitor analysis on Hanson. With forensic brilliance, he proved beyond reasonable doubt that Hanson's future advance depended on three key conditions.

1. It needed bigger and bigger acquisitions to fuel its growth. As Hanson's appetite grew, so did the size of victims necessary to feed it. Even if it swallowed the largest possible targets in the UK stock market, there would be no large prey left within five years.

2. If Hanson was to continue to offer a large premium for its bids, it needed to remain on a higher rating – its stock market value relative to its earnings – than its targets.

3. This is the most damaging: Iain showed that after acquiring a company Hanson tended to raise the price of its products. This immediately boosted profits, but at the expense of market share. The future stream of sales and profits would therefore decline. Nobody could see what was going on because Hanson kept on making larger and larger acquisitions, which produced further immediate gains.

When the stock market understood this pattern, Iain argued, it would realise that Hanson's future earnings growth couldn't last. When the penny dropped, Hanson's high rating of shares relative to profits would plummet.

Then Hanson would be unable to make further acquisitions, and the chickens − in the form of market share and profit declines working their way through from earlier acquisitions − would come home to roost. The slowing of profit growth − and possible future declines − would depress Hanson's rating further.

This brilliant analysis did not save the Imperial Group. Hanson's reputation was too high, and the attack on Hanson from Imperial's own consultants lacked some credibility. Yet all was not in vain. The defence forced Hanson to raise its bid greatly. Imperial shareholders got another £1 billion over and above the premium previously offered. In the longer term, Iain's predictions came to pass. As LEK's dissection of Hanson's earnings growth gradually gained acceptance, Hanson moved from an above-average market rating to one below average.

The defence work helped LEK, too. Though we lost Imperial as a client, we made a killing on the last few months' work. Management realised the very high value, not just of perhaps saving their jobs, but also of forcing a higher offer from Hanson. The defence of Imperial and other clients also established LEK's reputation with investment bankers. We were brought into several other high-profile defence cases over the next few years.

Best of all, the wheel of misfortune had given LEK a new strategy. Without realising it, we had created a new star category: strategic analysis of acquisitions. And not just to defend companies, but also to act for acquisitive companies, in analysing potential targets and demonstrating whether they could be profitably taken over.

The strategy was not flawless. One problem was intellectual

inconsistency. We knew that our best clients for acquisition analysis were the firms who were least suited to make acquisitions – namely, clients from outside the sector being targeted. The safest and usually best acquisitions are those that are 'close' to the bidder, targets in the same line of business where the scope for 'synergy' is greatest. 'Synergy' is a glamorous label for raising prices or cutting costs because you eliminate a competitor. Acquisitions of close competitors has much lower risks than taking over firms in a different business, because there is more 'synergy', and because the executives of the acquirer know the business, can run the target, and are less likely to make silly decisions once they gain control.

LEK's dilemma was that nobody wanted analysis of close competitors, whom they understood. They wanted analysis of less related targets, about which they knew little. These were usually bad acquisitions.

The other problem with a focus on bid work was its cyclicality. Takeover fever came and went. As time went on, unrelated acquisitions, which were our bread and butter, rightly went out of favour. For this reason, we were always hesitant to put all our eggs in the acquisition basket. Colleagues argued that 'pure strategy' – not related to takeovers – should always comprise half of our business.

It took us a while to realise that there was another type of client for acquisition analysis, one that was not cyclical, but growing all the time. This was the 'private equity' industry – people who invest in non-listed companies. A few decades ago, private equity was largely 'venture capital' – backers of new and young businesses like yours or mine. Increasingly, however, as funds have gravitated to private equity because of its superior returns, its investors have put money into bigger and bigger companies, including ones that they take off the stock market, rejuvenate, and often refloat at huge profits. LEK rapidly became a leader in analysis for UK-based private-equity firms.

The 'DNA' of LEK – its essential and distinctive character – snugly fitted the needs of private-equity houses. What they wanted was rapid bite-sized analysis to see if the deal would work. They didn't want elegant flannel or strategic opinions. They wanted hard numbers and accurate investigation, and they wanted it within a week. Speed, heavy quantitative skills, relentless pursuit of data, and forensic prowess to get to the bottom of obscure numbers – these were LEK's forte. Analysis for private-equity bidders was right up LEK's street.

After four years and a zigzag quest, LEK finally had stardom thrust upon it. We may draw five lessons from LEK's odyssey.

1. Imitation, even of a highly profitable and savvy player, won't lead to a star business. There are only two exceptions. One is geography – a player may be imitated in a new country or region where it is not present, and sometimes the advantage of being first and the differences in the local market's preferences can lead the imitator to a star position that can be defended even against the business imitated. The other exception is where the follower has more money or a *much* better approach than the originator.

2. Even people who think they are very smart and experienced in a particular market can go badly astray with

their strategy – even if they are 'strategy experts'! It is always easier to devise a great strategy for somebody else. Knowledge and confidence can blinker. It is very, very hard for someone inside a market to innovate fundamentally. The best innovators usually come from outside the mainstream market. This is great news for wannabe entrepreneurs.

3. The successful innovator's religion is *being different*. As different as possible, consistent with doing things in an economically sensible way – doing things that customers like but that are not expensive to do, and not doing things that are expensive yet don't have much customer appeal.

4. Disaster can turn to sweet outcomes if you experiment enough and listen to what the market is telling you.

5. If you don't have a star business now, that doesn't mean you can't have a star in the future. Where there is life, where there is enough cash to pay the bills, where there is the willingness to do something different, there is hope.

Conclusion

You don't have to be born a star. You can achieve stardom. But you won't become a star unless you aim to. You won't become a star unless you realise the importance of high market growth and niche leadership. You won't become a star unless you try out different approaches. You won't become a star unless you figure out what the market – via your ups and downs – is really telling you. Yet, if you are adventurous and ambitious, and understand the star idea, the odds for turning your venture into a star are surprisingly good. (Chapter 14 gives you some more specific hints on how to 'Evolve into a Star'.)

Whether your venture is born a star or becomes a star later, there is a common trail that all stars have blazed. By reverse-engineering this approach – working back from the successes to the common frame on which they were constructed – we can make it much easier and faster to become a star. That is what the next three chapters are all about. We're closing in on pay dirt.

8

Seven steps to heaven

To attain knowledge, add things every day. To attain wisdom, remove things every day.
Lao-Tzu

Acording to the Big Bang theory, one moment there was nothing and the next there was the start of the universe. Creating a new niche is not like that. It is more like creating a new species by mutating an existing one. First there are dinosaurs and then there are dinosaurs and birds. First there are apes and then there is *Homo sapiens*. This type of creation is much easier than starting the universe.

There are seven steps necessary for creating a star venture. The seven steps give you an easy template for devising your star.

Step 1: Divide the market. This takes an existing market and divides it into two. The baby niche will be tiny relative to the main market. No matter. What you are doing is dividing an existing market into two: everyone else's market and your new niche.

Step 2: Select a high-growth niche. This requires us to estimate future market growth in the possible niche. How confident can we be that it will grow at more than 10 per cent a year? Why? If we cannot be confident, we reject the idea and go back to Step 1 to select another niche.

Step 3: Target your customers. This step identifies the target customers' preferences. They must be clearly identifiable and different in profile from the customer needs in the main market. You must be confident that the product or service in the new niche will serve its customers' preferences much better than the existing market. Sometimes the customers will be different from those in the main market, but sometimes it is sufficient to meet the needs of customers in a different way (for example, sometimes the same consumer will drink Dr Pepper *and* Coke – as long as the consumer thinks of them as separate experiences and has loyalty to both).

Step 4: Define the benefits of the new niche. This specifies the benefits the new category provides over and above existing products in the main market. What it is offering more of? What is it offering that is better for the target customers? What is it offering that the main market doesn't provide at all? And also, what does the new product[8] not offer that existing products do? What is it subtracting from the main market?

Step 5: Ensure profitable variation. This step works out why the new niche can be more profitable than the existing market. If we aren't confident that varying the main

_____

[8] To avoid tedious repetition, where I write 'product' please read 'product or service'.

market will be more profitable – if we don't have good reasons why it will be – then we reject the idea and start again at Step 1.

Step 6: Name the niche you plan to lead. Unless you define your niche carefully, you cannot have a clear idea of who are your niche competitors – the firms you should really worry about – as opposed to firms in the main market, with which you compete only indirectly. Your profitability will be determined by whether you remain the niche leader and by how much, not by your share of the total market. At this stage, when you are having the idea for the new venture, you cannot ensure you retain niche leadership, but you can gain a head start by ensuring that your formula is difficult to copy. Make it difficult to understand the key differences behind your profits and growth. Do not reveal them or boast about them (until you have sold the business). Each day that passes, aim to increase the depth and reach of your formula and its difference from rivals or potential rivals, so that you become less like the main market and more distinctive than any niche competitors.

Step 7: Name the brand in a way that complements the category name. Make the name short, memorable, easy to recognise, appealing to the target market and associated with the niche.

Once you've completed the seven steps and feel good about the answers, you've created the new star enterprise *in your mind*. Nothing matters more. Everything else – creating the new enterprise in fact – is just putting flesh on the idea. If the idea is great – if it really is a star idea – you've *already* added the greatest value. If the idea is not great, no amount of skill in execution can make it a great business.

In the next chapter we'll go through the seven steps again so that you can use them to create your star idea. The rest of this chapter gives examples of the seven steps for three of my stars and three other well-known stars. The examples will give you the hang of the seven steps and give you confidence in them. If you're sure you understand the seven steps and are raring to get on with creating your own star, then skip the examples and move on to Chapter 9.

Betfair's Seven Steps to Heaven

Step 1: Betfair *divided* the betting market into the traditional market and the new betting exchange market.

Step 2: When Betfair started, its plan was predicated on rapid *growth* in the betting-exchange niche, because the benefits offered to customers were so great. On value alone, Andrew Black and his co-founder Ed Wray reckoned, it should be easy to find new customers who would rapidly shift most or all of their betting to the exchange. So it proved. When I invested, I had the benefit of several months' trading, showing month-to-month growth of more than 30 per cent. Subsequently, the betting-exchange market has grown enormously wherever it's been allowed to operate freely.

Step 3: Betfair's *target market* is professional gamblers and enthusiastic amateurs: people who bet big, often and intelligently – and often win. Traditional bookmakers close down winning accounts.

Step 4: The new niche offers three *benefits* to its target market. Above all, fair value. Next, the ability to bet against an outcome, to say it won't happen. Third, it allows users to trade bets – to reverse them or sell them when the odds change. What does the new niche not offer? It doesn't allow you to bet in a shop or at the track – you have to bet online or over the phone. Nor can you bet in cash. You have to register and deposit funds before you can gamble.

Step 5: The betting-exchange niche involves *profitable variation* because it does not require physical infrastructure – betting shops and staff. There is no need for people to set the odds. The cost of cash collection and payout is much lower. Betting exchanges offer greater value to customers while being more profitable to run.

Step 6: The *category name* – 'betting exchanges' is ideal. Short, simple, memorable, it sums up what the new category does: exchange bets between gamblers.

Step 7: 'Betfair' is a great *brand*, because it says clearly and succinctly what is the benefit of using the firm. 'Flutter' was a poor brand, connoting a casual wager undertaken purely for fun: not the target market at all.

Filofax's Seven Steps to Heaven

Step 1: Before Filofax came along, most people kept their personal details, appointments and addresses in a diary. Filofax *divided* the diary market into the main market and the personal-organiser niche.

Step 2: Filofax experienced two waves of high *growth* – in the 1980s, and again after we bought into the business in the early 1990s. From 1987 to 1990 nobody believed that the business could grow again. Everyone assumed that Filofax had been buoyed up by fashion and then cast down by it. My colleagues and I, however, saw a great brand that had inflicted needless harm on itself by escalating costs and prices. We saw a personal-organiser market alive and well, still growing at 10 per cent a year. We saw the possibility of regaining massive market share. Once again, this illustrates the wisdom of looking at the business and the category separately. Any business that has grown rapidly in the past may again grow rapidly in the future – with a different strategy.

Step 3: The *target market* was originally the professional classes, especially the church and the armed forces. In the early 1980s, the target market was widened to include yuppies, business people generally and women with demanding social lives. The personal-organiser market was a great deal more focused than the diary market.

Step 4: What *benefits* did personal organisers provide? Unlike a diary, they let the user collect together all relevant information and make notes at any time (since paper and pen were always present in the organiser) – to be visibly organised!

In the 1980s David Collischon gave Filofax another attribute – that of fashion accessory. With hindsight, this need would have been better served by developing a high-margin fashion line, keeping a lower-price organiser line. By moving the whole product line upmarket and letting prices get ridiculously high for those who wanted to be organised rather than admired, Filofax opened the door to lower-cost rivals.

Step 5: Personal organisers were more *profitable* than diaries because the benefits of an organiser were so much greater and therefore the loose-leaf 'infill' could be sold at much higher prices than a pad of paper. Given the unique six-hole configuration of a Filofax (later rivals either copied the Filofax format or invented their own one), customers had no choice. On the other hand, the convenience and efficiency of the personal-organiser system was such that customers who bought into the concept felt they were getting good value.

Step 6: When Filofax grew enormously in the 1980s as an expensive, aspirational product, the absence of a generic niche description became a problem for the leader. People began to use 'filofax' to describe the category, which meant that every competitor could describe their product as a filofax (note the lower case *f*). In 1986 David Collischon wisely coined the term 'personal organiser' to describe the category and encouraged everyone to use the term.

Marketing experts are adamant that it is easier for us to think first about a category generally, and then about the brand. 'I need a personal organiser to keep all my bits of paper. What brand should I ask for in the shop? Well, Filofax is the best known.' This is an easier and more natural way of thinking than, 'I need a Filofax.' The clear benefit of a *personal organiser* was that it helped people be *better organised*. If the term 'personal organiser' had not gained widespread currency the benefit of the new category would have been much less clear, and Filofax's brand name would have become devalued.

Contrast the confusion caused in the electronic-organiser niche. When this developed in the 1990s, the leading brand was PalmPilot. But what was the category name? As Al and Laura Ries comment, 'Some people call the Palm an electronic organiser. Others call the Palm a handheld computer. And still others, a PDA (personal digital assistant). All of these names are too long and complicated. They lack the clarity and simplicity a good category name should possess. If . . . a personal computer that fits on your lap is called a laptop computer, then the logical name for a computer that fits in the palm of your hand is a palm computer . . . Of course, Palm Computer pre-empted Palm as a brand name, leaving a nascent industry struggling to find an appropriate generic name . . . Palm Computer should have been just as concerned with choosing an appropriate generic name as it was in choosing an appropriate brand name.'[9]

---

[9] From their excellent book *The Origin of Brands* (New York: HarperCollins, 2004).

Step 7: Filofax is a great *brand* – simple, clear, yet with its own mystique. It was nicely complemented by the category name. If anyone asked, 'What do I do with a Filofax?' the answer was clear: it was a personal organiser, helping you become more organised. Without the niche name, the answer would have been much less apparent: 'It's a file of facts, get it?' Well, no, actually. The benefit of having a file of facts is not immediately evident. It was the same with Betfair. 'What does Betfair bring you?' 'The ability to *bet fair*.' That answer would not have been enough. Like all brilliant brands, 'Betfair' doesn't tell the whole story. But, if you understand what a betting exchange is, 'Betfair' adds a great twist and sums up the appeal admirably.

Belgo's Seven Steps to Heaven

Step 1: Belgo *divided* the UK restaurant market into 'the Belgo or similar-to-Belgo market' and all other restaurants. The new niche comprised Belgian restaurants with a monastery theme, different food and drink, and fast service.

Step 2: The niche *grew quickly*. Growth came from within each outlet as volume built, occupancy reached very high levels and the tables were turned ever faster. Major growth also came from opening new outlets.

Step 3: Belgo developed its own loyal *customers*, many dining at Belgo at least once a week. The core customers were creative professionals – PR and advertising executives, designers, media folk, architects, artists – in their thirties and forties. There was more than a whiff of the counterculture, rarely a tie in sight.

Step 4: What *benefits* did Belgo offer? According to the core customers, a unique experience, conviviality, unconventional glamour and excellent fast service.

Step 5: Belgo's *profitable variation* came from two things: its high gross margin from unique food and drink; and its high return on capital from turning the tables up to seven times a day, which in turn depended on factory-like organisation of production, high demand and customers' willingness to 'give back' the tables within 90 minutes. In turn, the high demand came from the buzz created by the two founders, by the heart and soul they put into the restaurants, the star quality that was impossible to define but equally impossible for customers not to recognise. The source of Belgo's profitable variation was not understood by the people who acquired the chain from us. Luke Johnson, the new chairman, was once filmed on 'reality television' working at Belgo. He was like an accountant at a rock concert. The new owners expanded to some places where the demand necessary to support Belgo's economics did not exist, and didn't realise the vital role of the founding duo in creating the buzz within and around each new Belgo. Once the duo split, the new outlets never built critical mass.

Step 6: The new *niche* was defined as 'restaurants like Belgo'. In fact, nobody copied the formula in its entirety, perhaps because the key role of fast production and delivery of food and drink was not appreciated. Because this was not apparent to would-be imitators, they struggled to make the sums add up and, where they did proceed, skimped on the design and fitting out of the restaurants. Nowhere else had the extravagant feel of Belgo, nowhere had the torrent of customer traffic, or was able to challenge Belgo in its category.

Step 7: The two founders devised a clever *brand* in Belgo. It attracted enormous free publicity from London journalists and food critics, reinforced by the idiosyncratic *Belgo Cook Book*, which featured the founders and poked fun at them.

McDonald's Seven Steps to Heaven

Step 1: In the beginning, before Dick and Mac McDonald instituted their 'speedee service system' for serving hamburgers in 1948, there was the coffee-shop market, where you could get coffee, cold drinks and a large variety of food. The McDonalds divided the coffee-shop market into the main market and their new niche, the fast-food hamburger restaurant. Long before Belgo, they pioneered a new menu and a new 'automated' way of delivering it.

Step 2: The brothers created a high-growth niche. Like Belgo, they grew by opening new restaurants and by rapidly expanding sales in their existing restaurants. Ray Kroc turbocharged the growth through franchising and international expansion. Since Kroc bought McDonald's in 1961, a majority of its restaurants have always been franchised, enabling rapid growth with little corporate capital.

Step 3: The target market was people who liked hamburgers. More recently the firm has targeted kids successfully. It was the first chain to provide a kiddie menu and playgrounds.

Step 4: The benefits for hamburger lovers are a reliable and consistent product that tastes the same every time and everywhere in the world; rapid service; and low prices. The 'speedee service system' multiplied the volume of hamburgers and fries, slashing the price for the ever-swelling flock of customers. Subtraction played a major part. The McDonalds subtracted the waiters and wait-resses. They eliminated most of the coffee-shop menu to focus on hamburgers and hamburger-related products. The menu shrank to nine items: hamburgers, cheeseburgers, fries and six drinks.

Step 5: Profitable variation: standardised procedures and speed made it possible to serve unprecedented numbers of meals for a restaurant of a given size. The high turnover made it possible to sell the meals very cheaply. The low price and consistent quality filled the restaurants.

By 1951, the San Bernardino shop grossed over $400,000 a year, around $3 million in today's money. That's double the sales made today by the average American McDonald's. With the cash thrown off, the brothers opened seven more restaurants in five years – much faster than Belgo! Their system changed the face of America and the world, making eating out a possibility for tens of millions of people.

The claim that Ray Kroc was the real founder of McDonald's is pure propaganda. Ray Kroc was a commercial genius. The most astute thing he did in his life was to buy a wonderful star business for far less than it was worth. His decisions to franchise and internationalise were visionary. But it was Dick and Mac who invented the formula for super-profitable growth.

Step 6: As well as always being the leading hamburger chain in the US, McDonald's was the first hamburger chain in nearly every European country and the first in most other countries in the world. It was the first global restaurant brand and has remained the largest. From 1948 to the early 1990s, McDonald's was the leader in a fast-expanding market.

Step 7: McDonald's has proved a great and enduring brand. The 'Big Mac' name for its most popular hamburger and the Golden Arches logo was inspired.

Cirque du Soleil's Seven Steps to Heaven

Step 1: Cirque du Soleil ('Circus of the Sun') divided the circus market into the traditional circus – everything up to then – and the new niche it created in 1984. Founded in Montreal by street performers, it created a 'reinvented circus' that uses a storyline for each performance, and imports artistic music and dance into the show. In some ways it's a cross between the circus and the theatre, with a dash of the opera, the ballet, rock music and busking!

Step 2: The new category grew rapidly, so that Cirque du Soleil attained within 20 years the same turnover as it took the leading traditional circuses – Barnum & Bailey and Ringling Bros – a century to build.

Step 3: The target customer of the circus is children. Cirque du Soleil targeted adults and corporate entertainment, and priced its performances at levels similar to those of the theatre, many times the circus price.

Step 4: The benefits offered by Cirque du Soleil were a unique entertainment experience with much greater coherence than the circus; great design, including an upgraded circus tent; comfortable seats; inspired use of colour; freshly composed music; and guest acts from the best veteran circus performers. The reinvented circus eliminated animal acts, the three-ring circus venues (multiple show arenas) and resident star performers.

Step 5: Cirque du Soleil's variations from traditional circuses are highly profitable. The most expensive parts of the circus – the animals and resident stars – were jettisoned, yet tickets are more expensive.

Step 6: Cirque calls its category 'the more modern circus'.[10] Cirque dominates its niche.

Step 7: Cirque du Soleil's brand has worked well, built by the quality of its performances and word of mouth.

---

[10] Interview with *Reveries* magazine, July 2002.

Coca-Cola's Seven Steps to Heaven

Step 1: John Stith Pemberton, a pharmacist from Georgia, invented a 'coca wine' in 1885. He called it Pemberton's French Wine Coca, and it sold reasonably well. When Atlanta went dry in 1886 he developed a fizzy non-alcoholic version, called it Coca-Cola and began selling it locally through soda fountains.[11] He divided the soft-drinks market into existing drinks – root beer, fruit drinks, sarsaparilla and so forth – and the new cola category he created. Pemberton divided another market too, since Coca-Cola was also sold initially as a patent medicine, able to cure headaches, nerves and depression. Coca-Cola was the first popular product that was both soda-fountain drink and patent medicine. Many great innovations simultaneously divide markets and combine the attributes of two previously unrelated markets.

Step 2: The cola category grew rapidly from the start. On 1 May 1887, the Atlanta Constitution reported that sales of Coca-Cola syrup in the past few weeks had been 600 gallons, equivalent to 76,800 drinks. In 1891 almost 20,000 gallons of Coca-Cola were sold. By 1895 this had reached 76,244 gallons, a compound growth of 40 per cent a year, and equivalent to nearly 10 million drinks. By 1900, Coca-Cola was already the most popular soft drink in America, a position held ever since.

---

[11] The first formulation of Coca-Cola used plain water rather than carbonated, until it was accidentally mixed with carbonated water. Customers much preferred the latter.

Step 3: The majority of early advertisements were aimed at businessmen, but three other groups were targeted: women, children and smokers.

Step 4: The benefits of Coca-Cola were initially medicinal: it was an 'ideal brain tonic and sovereign remedy for head-ache and nervousness'. Right from the start, also, Coca-Cola was touted as 'delicious and refreshing'. When the cocaine in Coke was cut out in the 1900s, marketing focused on Coke's taste and refreshing qualities. When cola competitors emerged, Coke stressed that it alone was 'the real thing'.

Step 5: Coca-Cola's *profitable variation* arose originally from its unusually high volumes as a drink sold through drug-store soda fountains. It benefited from the invest-ment already in place in the soda fountains. Like other soda fountain drinks, Coca-Cola sold for a nickel, but the ingredients cost less than half a cent. The issue, therefore, was not the percentage margin, but the absolute volume of sales and profit that could be generated. Asa Candler, who gained control of the company in 1888, boosted sales volumes through serious advertising. In 1892, Candler spent $11,400 on advertising, which was his major expense apart from the $22,500 spent on the ingredients. Candler also attracted new business from fountain owners by providing them with free drinks for new customers (who were given coupons) and with posters and promotional goods such as scales, cabinets, clocks and serving urns. Candler realised that advertising and local promotions could help to build a huge and profitable business, since the syrup's gross margin was so high. In building volume, Coca-Cola relied heavily on its medicinal claims, which differentiated it from virtually all other soda-fountain drinks.

Coca-Cola's other profitable variation arose serendipitously. For two years, Candler was pestered by an entrepreneur from Chattanooga, Benjamin Franklin Thomas, who wanted to bottle Coca-Cola. In 1889, Candler reluctantly agreed to Thomas's plan. The bottling of Coke was an instant success, leading to high profits for the company and bottlers. For Coca-Cola, bottlers created a huge new market without any capital need. By 1904 there were more than 120 bottling plants throughout the US. Coca-Cola may be the first example in history of a company concentrating on its 'core competencies' (in this case, product formulation, branding and marketing) and outsourcing all capital-intensive functions. As a result, the company grew enormously without having to raise much external capital. And it all happened by chance.

When competing colas emerged, Coke was able to command a substantial price premium. To this day, Coca-Cola has remained highly profitable. It currently has an operating margin of 26 per cent, instead of the 5 to 10 per cent typical in the food and beverage industry.

Step 6: Coca-Cola has been the number-one American cola ever since 1886. Coke was the first cola drink into most countries in the world and is the market leader in most countries too, with the notable exception of the Middle East, where Pepsi was first.

Step 7: Coca-Cola's apparently unshakeable dominance in the cola category it created has made it the most valuable brand in the world, worth $70 billion. That the cola category became so large and profitable is one of the minor commercial miracles of the twentieth century. It's an inspiration to entrepreneurs everywhere to expand their category's sales dramatically over the next century or so. If such value can be conjured from a sweet and sticky drink dreamed up by a tinkering druggist, think how much your category can grow – if you believe in it and have a long enough time horizon!

My favourite writers on brands and marketing, Al and Laura Ries, pose an intriguing challenge:

> What built the Coca-Cola brand? Was it a massive marketing program communicating the benefits of drinking Coke? Or was it that Coca-Cola pioneered the cola category?
>
> If creating a new category is the essence of brand building, then it pays to spend some time thinking where new categories come from.[12]

That is precisely what we are about to do, using our Seven Steps to Heaven as the template for you to create your new star business.

---

[12] *The Origin of Brands*, p. 174.

9

How to create your Star I

DREAMING UP STAR IDEAS

If you can dream it, you can do it.
Walt Disney

Introduction

This chapter and the next are the most important and potentially valuable in the book for you. If you use the chapters to create a good *idea* for your star, you will probably look back on that as a turning point in your life.

To start with, the idea is all in the mind. As with me when I sat in that deckchair in Brighton and had the idea about Filofax, the idea comes first. If it is a good enough idea, it's all downhill from there. If the idea is great, if it really is a star business in the making, then you already have determined success, even before you've done anything. If the star idea is sound, money to start the venture will come, customers will come, great staff will come, your fortune will come.

Although creating your star idea can be amazingly

rewarding, it's not difficult. The procedure is straight-forward, based on the Seven Steps to Heaven. In this chapter we work together to *generate a shortlist of two or three possible ideas* for the star venture by dividing existing markets into two – the current market and your new star niche. You will recognise this process as Step 1 in the Seven Steps to Heaven at the beginning of Chapter 8. In Chapter 9 we go on to *validate the ideas and choose one* of them as your star venture, following Steps 2 to 7.

The process requires a bit of inspiration, but it's fun. Team up with a good friend, or maybe two or three, to dream up potential star concepts together. The friends should be people you trust utterly and would like to do business with. They are your potential co-founders, so think carefully before you throw around the invitation to join you in some brainstorming.

You should all have read the book so far, paying particular attention to Chapter 8, then read this chapter on your own. If possible, each of you should come up with the germ of an idea or two. Schedule a couple of times to meet – two or three hours in the evening or at the weekend, when you're free and relaxed. Have a coffee or tea, a beer or a glass of wine if you like. If you don't find inspiration, leave it for a week or a month and come back to it. You may have the idea while you are cleaning your teeth or walking down the street.

Start with the markets you and your friends know. How could you turn them upside down, inside out, to create a new category?

Here are 32 useful *triggers*. Some of them are opposites, using one extreme or another to create a new niche. Go against the conventional wisdom of the main market. Many of these triggers are related or similar, but they are included just in case they prompt an idea that otherwise might not occur to you. Don't be overwhelmed by the list – it's there to help, not to hold you up. If you can't relate to a prompt, pass swiftly on to the next.

TRIGGER 1. YOUR IDEAL PRODUCT DOESN'T EXIST

The first trigger is the simplest. Is there a product or service you really want that is not available?

Andrew Black wanted a betting exchange, so that he could bet against other individuals and avoid giving book-makers excessive profits.

Karan Bilimoria wanted a 'less gassy' beer to drink with Indian food. His problem was that the lagers sold in Indian restaurants made him feel bloated, limiting the amount of beer and food he could consume. By combining the refreshing nature of lager with the smoothness of real ale, and selling it to accompany Indian food, he created Cobra, a star business with sales over £100 million.

On a more modest scale, I have written several books because I wanted one on the subject and couldn't find it. For example, I wanted a book on economist Vilfredo Pareto's '80/20 rule', to give to friends and business contacts. Although there were masses of articles on the subject available on the Internet, there was no book. *The 80/20 Principle* has been published in 25 languages and sold more than 700,000 copies.

Of course, you have to check that your taste is not unique, that there are enough 'people like you' to create a market in your gap. Surprisingly often there are.

TRIGGER 2. UPMARKET/DOWNMARKET

Could you create a luxury segment of the market? This is particularly fertile when nobody thinks much of the existing market, when it's a big Cinderella – dull, unprofitable, flat or declining.

The American retail coffee market used to fit this description to a T. Most coffee was sold in 'greasy spoon' cafés for around 50 cents. Then, around 1987, Starbucks started to open upscale coffee joints. Somehow, customers were inveigled into paying several times the price for exotic coffee in cool surroundings.

Now Starbucks has 10,000 coffee shops in 30 countries. Its sales are $6.4 billion and it's worth a very cool $29 billion.

Many great niches have been created with 'affordable indulgencies', a more expensive version of a cheap product. In their day, Coca-Cola and McDonald's both had aspects of the affordable indulgence.

What boring, barely profitable market do you know where you could imagine providing something much better for a multiple of the price?

Could you provide a high-end version of something that has traditionally been viewed as an economy product? What could be more low-end than prefabricated housing? Yet Champion Enterprises of Michigan has created a new niche of 'attractive prefabs' that can include features such as personalised skylights and fireplaces.

TRIGGER 3. AFFORDABLE LUXURIES

These are higher-ticket versions of 'affordable indulgencies'. Is there a really expensive product where you could create a new category that is much more affordable than the current luxury and yet retains high standards and much of its appeal?

Toyota created an extremely profitable new category with the Lexus. It's a luxury car with the performance of a BMW or Mercedes, but at a much lower price. Lexus comprises 3 per cent of Toyota's sales but a third of its profits.

Mazda took the same approach with the MX-5, the most popular sports car in the world. It has the performance of a low-end Porsche at half the price.

Business-class travel provides most of the benefits of first-class but at half the price. Some airlines, such as British Airways, make more than 100 per cent of their profits from business class and lose money on other cabins.

You may have an alligator shirt from Ralph Lauren. This is fashion without the fashion. It's a high-quality, classy garment that conveys the sense that you choose your clothes carefully. On the other hand, the look is classical and does not change over time. The result is enormous volume and much higher profits.

TRIGGER 4. MASS MARKET VERSUS NICHE

You could go a step further and create a genuine mass market where there is currently only a small, select market for rich people.

Before Henry Ford started mass-manufacturing cars, they were a luxury item for the very rich. Package holidays democratised the foreign-holiday market, which a generation or two ago was confined to the more affluent middle classes. Budget airlines such as Southwest, and in Europe

Ryanair and easyJet, have done something similar for independent travel. Fast-food restaurants made it possible to eat out for a fraction of the conventional restaurant tab.

Where is there a niche market only available to the well-heeled that could be turned into a mass market at a much lower price point? Define the category, define the price at which it could be a mass market and then engineer your costs to come in below that level.

There's always the possibility of an ultra-upscale niche. The fastest-growing part of the American economy (and many others) is that of millionaires, multimillionaires and billionaires. Between 1982 and 1999, the millionaire-plus American population tripled to 9 million, with a combined net worth of $30 trillion. The number of billionaires has soared from 13 in 1982 to at least 367 who have been counted publicly, and probably more than 1,000 when publicity-shy billionaires are added in. The Luxury Institute of New York conducted a survey of the best wristwatch brand among people with a net worth above $5 million. Cartier didn't make the top ten, Rolex just sneaked in and Breguet came only fifth. The clear choice of the rich was Franck Muller, a new Swiss brand, which does a brisk trade in watches over half a million dollars (though you can buy the cheapest one for a mere $5,000). Whatever luxury niches exist, there is always the potential to create one even higher, for surely in this market 'the more you pay, the more it's worth'.

Or go the other way. Is there is a mass market without an upmarket equivalent? If so, do a Starbucks. Food and drink products naturally lend themselves to luxury segments such as premium gin, super-premium gin, and pre-bought premium ready meals. Which foods or drinks don't have an upmarket segment? Why has nobody done a Starbucks with tea?

TRIGGER 5. BIGGER PRODUCT VERSUS SMALLER PRODUCT

New niches can be created by going bigger or smaller. Provide something bigger, more robust or more powerful – supersized McDonald's, 4 x 4 utility vehicles, sports cars.

Alternatively, make the product smaller – the wrist-watch, Dinky cars, Vespa scooters, Honda small motorbikes, personal computers, Volkswagens, Smart cars, mobile phones, Hewlett-Packard LaserJet printers, cherry tomatoes, Danone Actimel yoghurt.

Or go the whole hog and miniaturise – Matchbox cars, Sony Walkman, Palm computer, Leica camera, Game Boy video game, miniature Oreos and Snickers.

TRIGGER 6. EMOTIONAL VERSUS FUNCTIONAL

Emotion is warm and expensive. Function is no-nonsense, rational, inexpensive, stripped down to the essentials.

Can you create a new niche by going 'emotional' in a market that is mainly 'functional'? All premium brands – Belgo, Plymouth Gin, Filofax, Starbucks, Coke, designer clothes – take this route. So too, arguably, do organic foods, homeopathic remedies, and personal trainers – all major growth categories.

Or can you start a new category by going 'functional' in a mainly 'emotional' market? Microfile took away a swathe of Filofax's sales by providing a personal organiser that did exactly the same thing at half the price, only without the emotional baggage (English leather for the binder, the Filofax logo).

Stockbrokering, personal banking, insurance, tax advice and travel agency all used to be 'emotional' purchases. The wise personal stockbroker, the avuncular bank manager, the clued-up insurance broker, the trusted personal accountant and the friendly travel agent had comfortable premises. Most sales were made face to face. In every case niche innovators have provided products that are much cheaper, by stripping away the cost of face-to-face interaction using low-cost channels such as the phone and Internet.

TRIGGER 7. HEALTHIER VERSUS TEMPTING

The first project I undertook at LEK identified healthier food categories as *the* major growth market in that industry. That was in 1983. Since then the proliferation of new categories has amazed me. Half-fat, low-fat, non-fat, good-fat (polyunsaturates), reduced sugar, low sugar, sugar-free, low cholesterol, cholesterol-free, cholesterol-reducing, low acid, low salt, organic. Semi-skimmed milk, skimmed milk, everything in between. Health and whole-food shops.

The list goes on. Every year, major new categories are created and most of the healthier niches prosper. Tropicana created a lucrative star venture by inventing 'fruit juice not made from concentrate', giving us a new thing to worry about and pay to avoid. Another great new star is Silk, the dominant US supplier of soya milk, a new category it pioneered, growing at 50 per cent a year. (Never mind that the Chinese invented the drink around 164 BCE.) Why Silk? A brilliant contraction of *soya* and *milk*.

Another new star is Splenda, the first zero-calorie natural sweetener, invented by McNeil Nutritionals. Splenda dominates the niche it created and already has similar volume, built over decades, to Sweet'N Low and Equal, the two leading artificial sweeteners.

Whole Foods Market created the natural-food retailing category and is the dominant star in the American market, growing at 15–20 per cent a year. It is not too late for regional entrepreneurs, in Europe and Asia, to create similar star ventures.

Yet the food industry also evidences new star ventures from the creation of *less healthy* niches, such as luxury ice cream (really 'double-fat'), chocolate-laden desserts (the aptly named Death by Chocolate), and high-sugar or super-caffeinated drinks. Ben & Jerry's ice cream was founded in 1978 in a converted petrol station in Vermont with $8,000 capital and borrowings of $4,000. It rapidly became a star. The firm was sold to Unilever in 2000 for $326 million, nearly 41,000 times the starting capital. Jerry Greenfield got $19 million, Ben Cohen $46 million.

These sums are chickenfeed, however, compared with money made from Red Bull, a superstar venture founded nine years after Ben and Jerry's. Red Bull created and dominated the *energy drink* category (a carbonated high-sugar, high-caffeine drink) and now sells well over 2 billion cans a year. Red Bull GmbH is a private company so it's difficult to value, but with sales of $2 billion and high profit margins it must be worth several billion dollars. Founder Dietrich Mateschitz is the richest Austrian alive.

If you're thinking of creating a new star within the food

and beverage industries, *healthier* and *tempting* are still useful prompts.

TRIGGER 8. SAFE VERSUS RACY

If you want a safe car, chances are you'll pick a Volvo, the car manufacturer that pioneered the category of 'safe cars'. If you want something racier and can afford it, perhaps a Ferrari? With its wide seat and canopy, a BMW is a relatively safe motorbike. The racy buy is Harley-Davidson. If you can't afford a Harley bike, they'll kindly sell you a (rather expensive) Harley bike jacket. Racy is pricey and profitable.

Could you pioneer a safe or racy segment in the industry you're reviewing?

TRIGGER 9. CONVENIENCE VERSUS PURITY

Create a star through inventing a new, more convenient category. Nescafé instant coffee. Cliff's Notes. 3M's Post-it Notes. Filofax personal organisers. Teflon non-stick frying pans. Dyson bagless vacuum cleaners.

It's more difficult to create a segment through appealing to purists who value authenticity even at the expense of convenience. Authentic segments are difficult to create from scratch.

By creating much larger bookstores with depth of range, comfortable seats, knowledgeable staff and coffee shops, Borders and Barnes & Noble managed the difficult feat of combining convenience with purity.

TRIGGER 10. SAVING TIME VERSUS EXTENDING TIME

With life appearing to accelerate beyond our control,

saving time is a great way to create a new star. Witness the evolution of mass-market food from the diner to the automat to McDonald's. Half a century later we created a new niche with Belgo, not fast food, but *faster* restaurants. High-speed trains. Private jets. ATMs. Self-service in all its forms, including self-service supermarket checkouts.

On the other hand, extending time is also a viable differentiator. Make the bookshop comfortable and you'll start reading a book and then buy it. Make Starbucks a place to meet colleagues and hang out. Why did first class win out against Concorde? Apart from the poor economics of supersonic travel, customers preferred a luxury and spacious crossing to a cramped and noisy experience in half the time.

TRIGGER 11. FIXED VERSUS MOBILE
Stationary versus on-the-run. Sure, this has been done in fast food and mobile phones, with the Sony Walkman and the Apple iPod. Could it be done elsewhere? Of course it can. Imagination is the only constraint.

TRIGGER 12. UNISEX VERSUS SINGLE SEX
Unisex was seventies. Single sex is noughties and will be 2010s. In 1995 Curves created a new star venture with health clubs exclusively for women. It's now the world's largest fitness franchise with 10,000 clubs, 4 million members, and revenues of $2.6 billion. A new Curves opens somewhere in the world every four hours – this star will grow and grow.

How could you create a new star by focusing exclusively on men or women?

TRIGGER 13. MASCULINE VERSUS FEMININE

This is not the same as gender-specific ideas. Marlboro created a star by taking the 'masculine cigarette' market-space. Almost half Marlboro smokers are women. As the great psychologist Carl Jung stressed, men need to express their feminine side and women their masculine inclinations.

Many new stars could be created by crafting masculine or feminine identities for products and services.

TRIGGER 14. GO GAY

'Why not a gay gym chain?' I asked a friend. 'All gyms are gay,' he replied. I'm not so sure.

Some products are directly targeted at gay men – often a sustainable and profitable niche. Calvin Klein underwear ads appear to be deliberately homoerotic.

TRIGGER 15. GO GREY

The over-50s/60s market is growing and well heeled. The obvious markets such as retirement homes and 'sheltered accommodation' are less interesting than the possibility of creating new grey segments within existing large markets. In the UK Saga ('serving people aged 50 and over') has done this brilliantly, selling holidays, insurance, and homes in Spain. Many other mainstream markets don't yet have a grey specialist.

Here some possibilities to ponder:

★ Fashion: how does the Gap/Boden generation grow old stylishly?

★ Education: universities for those aged 50-plus?

★ Clubs: where to socialise disgracefully without being patronised by younger members?

★ Sex and dating: is a specialist site long overdue?

★ Technology support for the IT-excluded or defeated?

★ Senior cosmetics, toiletries, luxury foods, fitness centres?

★ A social networking site similar to MySpace but focused on mature people?

★ Music and concerts targeted at golden oldies?

What market do you know well where you could create a grey star venture?

TRIGGER 16. LOW VERSUS HIGH SERVICE, AND *DIFFERENT* SERVICE

If the industry you're reviewing is a high-service one, go low service or no service. If it provides predominantly low or poor service, think of a new category with great service.

Equally, you can focus on a particular set of customers who have different requirements. They may not require high service as the industry has traditionally defined it, and they may be prepared to do some of the work that the suppliers have always provided – thus leading to substantial cost savings. On the other hand, this particular group of customers may have other needs that you can supply, thus providing a service that is *cheaper and better* for this group of customers.

The French-based Formule Un hotel chain is targeted at budget-conscious customers who want nothing more or less from a hotel than a good night's sleep. There are limited check-in times and limited services (concierge, room service, food and so forth), but there is always a comfortable bed and excellent noise insulation.

In the home-furniture market, IKEA has become the international leader with a global network of more than 100 huge stores, targeted at younger customers who appreciate simple Scandinavian style and low prices, and are willing to spend time selecting, transporting and assembling the furniture themselves. IKEA has 'destination' stores that require a special trip, but the formula includes ample free parking, kids' play areas, cafés, excellent product information and tape measures.

A very interesting innovation – sure to spread elsewhere – is the UK company Glasses Direct, which sells glasses and contact lenses online at a fraction of the price charged by conventional opticians. Glasses Direct encourages customers to get an eye test at a high street/main street optician, then buy online using that prescription. By piggybacking off the premises and staff of conventional opticians, Glasses Direct is able to offer glasses for an eighth of the price charged by the former (£17.50 versus nearly £150). The customer has to do a little more work but avoids paying through the nose. The conventional optician chains are stumped, unless they start charging the full cost for eye tests, and no chain wants to be the first to make that move.

Could you change the service 'menu' in a particular industry? Could you eat into someone else's market share by doing something similar to Glasses Direct?

TRIGGER 17. DIY VERSUS PROFESSIONAL SERVICE

If you're thinking about a particular professional service, and there isn't a do-it-yourself alternative, could you provide it?

Fifty years ago you hired a craftsman to improve your home, or you went to the local hardware store for a hammer and some nails. There wasn't much in between. Now there is a vast home-improvement industry, with out-of-town sheds like aircraft hangars to sell you everything you could possibly need in order to do it yourself.

Thirty years ago you worked out your taxes with paper, pencil and calculator, or you hired a tax accountant to do it for you. Now you can use Intuit's Quicken financial software. Founded in 1983, Quicken is still a star, having beaten off determined competition from Microsoft. Intuit is worth some $12 billion.

TRIGGER 18. PERSONALISED VERSUS UNTAILORED

Everything can be personalised, and, sooner or later, everything will be. The *personal* computer opened the floodgates. If your industry has empty spaces for personalised products, your star awaits.

Dell Computer supplies *personalised* personal computers direct and does nothing else.

TRIGGER 19. BUNDLED VERSUS FOCUS AND SUBTRACTION

In a new category, especially with newly defined customers, a bundled service can create a new star business. Zeneca did this with its Salick cancer centres in the USA, pulling together all treatments that patients might need. Arguably, Microsoft pulled the same trick with its Microsoft Office and Microsoft Explorer (though some would claim that Microsoft simply sought to reinforce its niche monopoly with whatever products were needed).

On the other hand, when an industry leader provides a broad range of products or services, there is usually scope for a specialist who provides the very best in one product or service area, and does nothing else.

Focus is by far the best way to create a new star venture. Compaq did this in personal computers for businesses. Intel, now the world's fifth most valuable brand, built its fortunes exclusively on the microchip. Intel made the first microchip and was so committed to its new star venture that it closed down its computer-memory chip operations to focus totally on microprocessors.

Kevin Plank, a University of Maryland athlete, created his star venture, Under Amour, by pioneering the 'athletic underwear' segment, with garments designed to minimise sweat saturation.

Boston Chicken created a new star venture by selling takeaway rotisserie chicken. When Boston Chicken diversified into other meats and became Boston Market, the slide to oblivion began. Boston Chicken began by *subtracting* other meats and prospered. Boston Chicken ended by *adding* other meats, and perished.

McDonald's began by *subtracting* the coffee-shop menu not related to hamburgers, and prospered. McDonald's has done much less well since it started adding chicken, salad and other items to its menu.

Subtraction is an incredibly powerful way to create a star venture. BlackBerry took the personal computer and subtracted everything but the e-mail function. Result: a mobile e-mail machine and a great star venture.

What new category can you create by focus and subtraction?

TRIGGER 20. EXPERT VERSUS INEXPERT USERS

Mainframe computers had to be used by qualified computer programmers; but even I can use a personal computer.

Financial calculations used to require experts to manipulate slow and complex programs. VisiCalc invented the computer spreadsheet, accessible to any professional. Lotus Development Corporation then introduced a more powerful spreadsheet, Lotus 1-2-3, which could be run on any IBM-compatible machine (VisiCalc could only be used on the Apple II). Lotus quickly became the spreadsheet star; this one product made Lotus dominant and, for several years, larger and more profitable than Microsoft.

Wine used to be intimidating, but popular brands have made it accessible.

The bestselling books . . . *for Dummies* have taken the fear out of learning.

Do you know a category where existing products or services require too much knowledge from the user to tap a mass market?

TRIGGER 21. CENTRALISED VERSUS DECENTRALISED USE

Accessing inexpert users – always a larger potential pool of customers – often goes along with decentralising the way that a product is used. In the days when Xerox dominated photocopying, the machines were often kept in a centralised service department. Gestetner sold much cheaper duplicating machines that could be used in any small office. Then Canon and Ricoh completed the circle by selling small plain-paper copies as cheaply as duplicators, sending that market into terminal decline.

TRIGGER 22. TOTAL COST VERSUS INITIAL PRICE

Buses used to be bought on the basis of the price of the bus. The cheapest tender won. The problem with that was that municipal authorities often ended up with clunky, uncomfortable rust buckets emitting foul fumes and often breaking down. Repairs, maintenance, downtime and fuel use often meant that a cheap bus cost more in the end than a better bus. Enter North American Bus Industries (NABI), pioneering buses made from fibreglass rather than steel. NABI argues that its lighter buses cost much less to run, give more space inside the bus, require much less maintenance and are more 'green' to boot.

TRIGGER 23. FIRST PLACE VERSUS THIRD PLACE

The first place is home, the second is work and the third is the place to relax and meet people. The club, bar, pub, church.

If the market you want to enter serves the home, could you create a category by shifting product use to the 'third place'? Starbucks began by selling coffee beans for home grinding, before realising that the 'third place' – a chain of sit-down retail stores – offered much greater profit.

Other innovators have moved a product from the 'third

place' to the 'first place', for example by selling gourmet ready meals to cook at home. Domino's became a star by being the first large chain to provide home delivery of pizza. Papa Murphy's has found another route to stardom, providing 'half-baked' pizzas to be finished in the oven at home. In video rental, Blockbuster has become the dominant star almost everywhere.

Instead of gyms, why not home exercise programmes?

TRIGGER 24. SECOND PLACE VERSUS THIRD PLACE

A small business I know that rents a serviced office and has to pay for conference rooms sends its people to Starbucks to have meetings! Video-conferencing substitutes the workplace for third-party conference hotels. Can you think of another innovation that substitutes a third-party location for the workplace, or the other way round?

TRIGGER 25. OWNED VERSUS RENTED VERSUS FRACTIONALLY OWNED

If the industry standard is to rent machines, could you create a new category by selling them instead? When Xerox insisted on leasing plain-paper copies, Canon sold them. In Britain, Margaret Thatcher gained enormous political advantage by selling rented 'council' houses at knockdown prices, enabling millions of ordinary people to own a home.

Now the hot ticket to innovation is fractional ownership. It was done with holiday timeshares. Now it is ripe for any really expensive asset.

In 1986, NetJets began selling fractional ownership of private jets. For a current price of $406,250, firms can buy one-sixteenth of a jet, giving 50 hours of flying time a year. For any but the largest of firms it makes sense to own a fraction of a private jet rather than a whole plane, giving the timesaving and flexibility of using a private plane when it is really needed at a cost often not much greater than using commercial airlines. NetJets is still a high-flying star, with revenues of $3.7 billion, growing over 30 per cent a year.

TRIGGER 26. NARROWED EXPERTISE VERSUS ADDED EXPERTISE

If you want to sell a professional service, this prompt is for you. Should you subdivide the area of expertise, or add expertise from another area to create a new service?

Either, or both, can be a real winner. Most new professional-services categories originated by narrowing the focus, taking one market and dividing it into two. For example, 50 years ago there were public-relations agencies but no specialist 'investor-relations' agencies to market a listed company to the investment community. Ten years ago the investor-relations category was split again, with specialist agencies focusing purely on online investor relations.

Bain Capital became the most successful venture-capital firm by combining the traditional expertise of venture capitalists with the know-how of strategy consultants.

Going further back, the Boston Consulting Group both narrowed and broadened its area of expertise. It created the first 'strategy consultancy' by narrowing the focus of its consulting to purely intellectual strategy issues. On the other hand, it created a new area of expertise by combining two skills that had previously been separate: financial expertise and market analysis.

When Bill Bain left BCG to found Bain & Company, he found another way to narrow and broaden the focus simultaneously. Bain & Company narrowed the focus to work only for CEOs and declining to work for more than one client in an industry. But Bain & Company widened their area of work to include cost reduction as well as 'pure' strategy, seeing that both areas were essential to boost the bottom line.

TRIGGER 27. ORCHESTRATING A SUPPLIER ALLIANCE

In 1996 AbeBooks of Victoria, Canada, created a star business by persuading four bookshops to let it market their used books online. Today, AbeBooks is the world's leading supplier of used, rare and out-of-print books, listing over a million titles from 13,500 booksellers.

TRIGGER 28. ONLINE VERSUS OFFLINE, OR A DIFFERENT DISTRIBUTION CHANNEL

People talk about the Internet bubble of the late 1990s, but what amazes me is how many great new star businesses are *still* being created by online innovations. The flow rolls on: many acquaintances are developing fresh ideas. It's not too late.

Conceptually, of course, the Internet is just another channel of distribution. New star businesses can also be created by imaginative focus on one or more particular channel of distribution, such as the phone, mail order (combined with the Internet) and direct sales.

TRIGGER 29. ENTREPRENEURIAL JUDO

This is a different kind of prompt, courtesy of the management guru Peter Drucker. The idea is to catch the leading players in a market off balance by turning their strength into a weakness. If you go back a generation or two, the best sites for shops in most cities and towns were smack bang in the centre. They had the best location and shoppers flocked there. Now, the best place to be is miles away, in the new shopping malls. By providing easy access by car, and lots of parking, the malls turned the old high street/main street locations, once a great asset, into an expensive liability.

In Belgium, Kinepolis has applied the same idea to movie theatres. Nearly all traditional cinemas are located in city centres, which used to be their strength. Kinepolis turns this advantage on its head. It provides a massive 'megaplex' off the Brussels ring road, with free parking, 7,600 huge seats, 25 screens and lower prices. Yet it makes a lot of money, because of low rent and high customer throughput.

In the market for retail scales (to weigh goods in shops), the market leaders in the 1970s were firms that had extensive service networks, so that if the scales in a store broke down they could be fixed or replaced immediately. This advantage was turned into a disadvantage in the 1980s by new firms providing electronic scales, which cost less and didn't break down. The service networks turned into a big problem, stopping the leaders from selling electronic scales until it was too late.

If you know a market well, can you think of a way to make the leaders' advantage an albatross?

I've saved three of the best prompts until the end.

TRIGGER 30. GO GREEN

'Green' is one of the best ways of creating a new category, since it latches on to a growth trend that will last for decades and even, if humans survive, for centuries.

In 1976, a mother burdened with kids, but without any business training or experience, opened the first Body Shop outlet on a green ticket, selling cosmetics produced in an ecologically sustainable way and not tested on animals. Green stores. Green products – all products are unique house brands, and all have some green theme, such as soaps and shampoos based on natural fruits and herbs. The Body Shop became a terrific star business, growing 50 per cent a year for two decades, marketing purely through social and environmental activism. Today it has 1,980 stores serving 77 million customers in 50 countries. In 2006 L'Oréal bought the Body Shop for £652 million ($1.2 billion).

High-quality natural clothing is a green market where there are many unoccupied niches. For example, it wasn't until 1995 that anyone thought of using the wool from merino sheep to provide designer active outdoor wear. Merino wool is an incredible natural fibre – thinner and stronger than ordinary wool, breathable, warm in winter, cool in summer, it doesn't hold odour, and has the athletic performance of the world's best dry-fit sportswear but is not made with oil. Jeremy Moon founded Icebreaker in Wellington, New Zealand, and it now supplies 1,500 stores in 22 countries.

Recycling offers immense potential and many such ventures are unusually attractive because they are natural monopolies within their catchment area, and hence almost certainly star businesses. A good example is Closed Loop, a patented Australian system for recycling food-grade plastic waste and providing it to food retailers. Closed Loop plants are going up all around the world, the latest being one in Dagenham, near London.[13]

One of the best sources of new green business ideas is to be found on Springwise.com.[14] Recent ideas include:

★ EarthFriendlyMoving, a company in California that rents environmentally friendly crates for moving, including 'poopy pallets' made from recycled baby diapers/nappies;

★ Sydney-based Todae, which consults to businesses to reduce their use of energy and water;

★ BottleCycler, another Australian venture, which helps the hospitality industry recycle glass bottles;

★ Ozocars, the first fleet of taxis to use environmentally friend cars (mainly 'hybrid' electric/petrol vehicles); these are popping up all over the world, along with 'green' car rental services;

---

[13] UK investors can gain exposure to Closed Loop through investment in Foresight 2, 3, or 4 Venture Capital Trusts. Declaration of interest: I am a non-executive director of Foresight 3 VCT.

[14] See http://www.Springwise.com/eco_sustainability.

★ a gym in Hong Kong that uses exercise machines to power lighting;

★ vinyl-free wallpaper;

★ recyclable carpets;

★ recycled paper hangers (most wire hangers end up in landfill);

★ 'green' weddings.[15]

A wise proverb says, 'Doing good is good business.' Going green is one of the best ways of creating a new star venture. The number of vacant green niches, for retailers, manufacturers and service providers, is stupendous. But look lively. The gaps won't last long.

TRIGGER 31. IDEAS FROM OTHER INDUSTRIES

Identify an industry that has a peculiar practice that somehow seems to work well. Could you adapt the practice to a completely different context?

If you'd done the exercise a decade or so ago, you might have identified the rarefied world of art dealing. Art dealers are eccentric – they sell by *auction*. There is something about getting qualified buyers in a room for a few minutes, forcing them to bid against each other. It produces consistently high prices, sometimes ridiculously so. Incredibly lucrative for the likes of Sotheby's and Chris-

---

15 More detail on all of these is available from http://www.Springwise.com.

tie's, who earn commissions totally unrelated to their costs. (Incidentally, Samuel Baker created Sotheby's as a new star business on 11 March 1744, when he auctioned several hundred rare books.)

About forty years ago investment bankers learned the same trick. They made hostile takeovers into auctions.

If you had used the auction idea before 1995 and applied it to online selling, you might have founded eBay.

The potential of auctions as a tool to create star ventures is far from exhausted.

If you had applied the idea of stockbroking to another industry before 2000, you might have founded Betfair.

TRIGGER 32. IDEAS FROM OTHER PLACES

A huge number of billion-dollar stars have been created by copying or adapting ideas from other cities or countries.

Anita and Gordon Roddick had the idea for the Body Shop when they came across a similar shop in Berkeley, California, selling shampoos, lotions and body creams. The name of that store? It was called – wait for it – the Body Shop.

Dietrich Mateschitz had the idea for his star business when he saw tuk-tuk drivers in Thailand drinking a local brew called Krating Daeng. This means 'Red Bull', as perfect a brand name in English as in Thai. He simply patented that brand, licensed and adapted the product, and promoted it as the first 'energy drink'.

Howard Schultz saw trendy coffee shops in Milan selling a variety of coffee and espresso products and decided that Starbucks should emulate them. At the time Starbucks sold only coffee beans and equipment, and the owners rejected

Schultz's idea. Schultz left Starbucks to start a chain of coffee bars called Il Giornale. Soon after, he bought Starbucks and rebranded his outlets as Starbucks.

Many entrepreneurs have created great star ventures just by copying ideas from America. The entire European and Asian venture-capital and private-equity industry falls in this category, as do most of the rest of the trillion-dollar financial-services industries outside the US.

Australian Janine Allis saw juice bars in America and cobbled together AU$250,000 from friends to open her own version in Adelaide. Seven years later, Boost Juice Bars are a great star business, with more than 170 stores in Australia and outlets in Chile, Indonesia, Kuwait and Singapore.

A round-the-world plane ticket could prove a fantastic investment. If you look creatively you are bound to find an idea for a great new star venture. Who knows? Your idea too could become worth billions.

Conclusion

Make a shortlist of your star ideas and try to reduce them to the two or three ideas that are strongest (if opinions differ, there's no harm having up to five ideas on the shortlist). Great! That's enough work for today's session. Now fix another meeting to *validate* the ideas and choose your star idea.

10

How to create your Star II

VALIDATING AND CHOOSING YOUR STAR VENTURE

If you have built castles in the air, your work need not be lost . . . Now put the foundations under them.
Henry David Thoreau

Are you and your friends sitting comfortably? Then we'll begin. In your last session (Chapter 9) you selected a shortlist for your star idea, Step 1 of the Seven Steps to Heaven. Now let's evaluate the shortlist against the six remaining steps.

Step 2: Select a high-growth niche

Do all the ideas on your shortlist promise growth for many years of at least 10 per cent a year? If you have doubts, scrub the idea.

The higher the likely growth, the better. Over ten years, annual growth of 30 per cent is more than five times better than growth of 10 per cent. Annual growth of 50 per cent is more than 22 times better, and 70 per cent is nearly 78 times better than 10 per cent!

Even more vital than the growth rate is how long it lasts. Annual growth of 20 per cent over 20 years is better than growth of 30 per cent over ten years (nearly three times better), while growth of 50 per cent over 20 years is much better than growth of 70 per cent over ten years (over 16 times better).

High growth sustained long enough creates amazing value. If you start with sales of just $100 in Year One and you grow by 50 per cent for 30 years, you end up with sales topping $19 million. Assume a 15 per cent return on sales and that the business is worth 15 times pretax profits, that is $43.5 million. Roll that forward another decade and it becomes $2.5 billion.

As an indicator of possible sales and profit growth, ask yourself these questions.

★ *How large is the market that your niche will substitute into?* If you are Betfair, that's the world's betting market. For Belgo, it was large but much more modest – the London market for restaurant food costing around £20 a head.

★ *How much of that market could you possibly hope to gain eventually?* For Belgo, perhaps 1 per cent at most. For Betfair, the figure is much larger – maybe 50 per cent.

★ *How clear is the definition of the target customers and how confident are you that they will prefer your new niche to the existing market?*

★ *How compelling are the benefits of the new product to the target customers, compared with what they enjoy at the moment?*

★ *How profitable will leadership in the new niche be? Why is the variation caused by the new category profitable? How much more profitable will leadership in the new niche be, relative to leadership in the existing market?*

Step 3: Target your customers

The narrower the target customer focus, the easier it is to market the service, and to be confident the new niche will work.

Andrew Black *knew* that people like him would love a betting exchange.

Bill Bain *knew* that ambitious and insecure CEOs would love Bain & Company's service.

When Michael Dell was a student at the University of Texas, he *knew* that people like him would love the personal computer systems he tailored to the customer's requirements and sold directly. The company he founded in 1984 with $1,000 has evolved into the world's largest direct seller of computers, worth $54 billion – a 54-million-times increase!

Sometimes, it's true, a customer focus emerges only over time. It can even be accidental, the result of unforeseen market feedback. In the late 1960s, sales of Honda's small scooters took off after people in Los Angeles saw the firm's employees riding them and demanded to buy one – it had never occurred to Honda that Americans would buy the tiny bikes they sold in Japan. When we opened Belgo, we did not know that our core customers would be creative professionals.

Yet if you are deciding between possible new star ideas, or deciding whether or not to launch a new venture, having a clear idea of the target customer is very important. The fuzzier the focus, the less chance of success.

Next, be crystal clear *why* they will prefer the new niche to the main market . . .

Step 4: Define the benefits of the new niche

We cannot create a new star without creating a new category. The new niche must be oriented towards the target customers and must offer a *sharply different basket of benefits* from the main market. The more the benefits of the new category vary clearly and substantially from the existing market, the greater the chance that the new venture will fly.

There are three ways of varying the benefits:

★ **increasing** one or more benefits of the product in the main market to a marked degree;

★ **creating** one or more new benefits that do not currently exist in the main market; and

★ **subtracting** benefits that exist in the main market.

Subtracting benefits is important because it usually enables the new category to lower costs, and/or to substitute the new benefits without charging more, because of the saving on the benefits subtracted. Subtracting benefits is also useful to differentiate sharply the new category from the main market, and to make it clear that it is for a different kind of customer. Subtracting is sometimes the essence of the innovation. Algebra created a new branch of mathematics by subtracting the numbers. Fast food created a new category of restaurant by subtracting the waiters. TaB (and later Diet Coke) created a new category of cola by subtracting the sugar.

Ideally, pursue all three ways of varying the market, with the target customers in mind:

★ **increasing** the benefits that really matter to the target market;

★ **creating** new benefits that will appeal strongly to the target market; and

★ **subtracting** benefits that are unimportant to the target market.

Betfair

★ dramatically *increased value for money* in the betting market;

★ provided the *new benefits* of being able to bet against outcomes, being able to trade bets and guaranteeing that winning accounts would not be closed; and

★ *subtracted* the ability to bet in retail premises or at the track, or to bet and collect winnings in cash.

Betfair's target market is big gamblers: professionals and serious enthusiasts. The change in profile between what betting exchanges offered and what the main market offered was ideally suited to the target market.

★ Getting great value is essential if a gambler is to win. It is very difficult to win if the bookmaker takes out 20 per cent on each event. If a betting exchange takes out only 1 per cent, a serious gambler has to be only slightly more than 1 per cent more accurate than the market and he will win.

★ It is much easier to bet against an outcome and win than it is to specify the winner. (If there are eight horses in a race and the gambler has a strong view against the favourite, he can back against that horse without knowing which of the other seven will win.) Big gamblers are much more likely to bet against events than small gamblers. Big gamblers are also skilful in trading bets, which can be a risk-free way of making money. Finally, big gamblers are the only people whose accounts are regularly closed down by bookmakers.

★ Big gamblers do not frequent off-track betting shops and are more than happy to bet online and by phone, and to receive payment by bank transfer.

CONSTRUCT YOUR COMB CHART
This is a great way of displaying the extent to which the new category has different benefits from the existing market, and the extent to which the new category suits

a particular target customer group better.

First, define the 'purchase criteria' of the market as a whole – what, on average, are the important benefits for the customer. Figure 10.1 shows these for the betting market in the UK, using a 1 to 5 scale, where 1 is totally unimportant and 5 is vital:

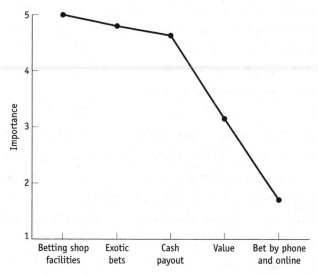

Figure 10.1 Betting market purchase criteria

The most important criterion in the UK mass betting market is the attractiveness of the betting-shop facilities: the TV screen to show races, racing newspapers showing the form, light and spacious premises. Almost as important are 'exotic bets' – the ability to place bets such as accumulators (where you back several horses and make a fortune if they all win) and forecasts (not just the winner but the second and so on) – and immediate cash payout if you win. Of rather less importance to the mass market is the value provided by the bookmaker. Finally the ability to bet by phone and online does not matter much in the main market.

Now we can see how far the existing suppliers (before you invent the new niche) satisfy these criteria. Figure 10.2 shows how the UK mass market rates the performance of the big bookmakers against their purchase criteria. You will see that the bookmakers perform well on all criteria except value, where they are rated slightly below the importance of the criterion.

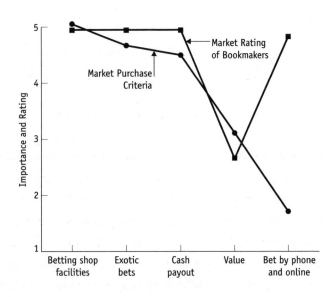

Figure 10.2 Rating of traditional bookmakers
relative to market purchase criteria

Now comes the fun part. We create a chart like Figure 10.1, but instead of drawing it for the main market, we draw it for the *target customers* we have in mind. Andrew Black's target customers were people like him – big, sophisticated gamblers.

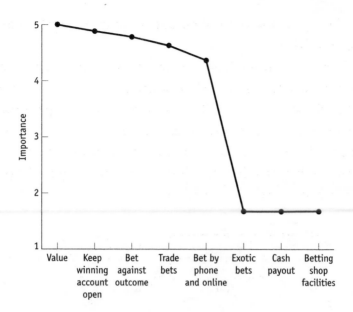

Figure 10.3 Purchase criteria of big gamblers

Figure 10.3 shows how much the big gamblers differ from the main market in what is important for them. The most important things for the big players are value; keeping winning accounts open; being able to bet against an outcome; trade bets; and betting by phone and online. All of these are unimportant for the main market with the exception of value, which is only moderately important. And the three most important criteria for the main market – betting shop facilities, exotic bets and cash payout – don't matter to the big gamblers.

Figure 10.4 completes the picture. Here we super-impose on the purchase criteria of the big gamblers their rating of both the traditional bookmakers and of betting exchanges.

We can see an almost perfect fit between what the big

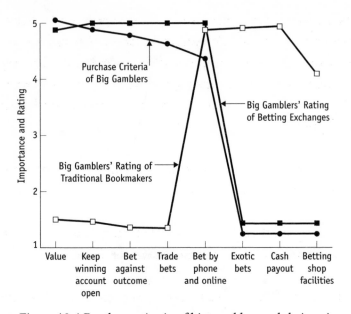

Figure 10.4 Purchase criteria of big gamblers and their rating
of traditional bookmakers and betting exchanges

gamblers want and what betting exchanges provide, which
is in marked contrast to the terrible fit between the big
gamblers' criteria and their rating of traditional bookmakers.

Whenever there is a picture like Figure 10.4, you can be
confident that the new category will take off, because it
meets the purchase criteria of a group of customers who
don't like what they are being offered now.

Did Betfair do this analysis before it launched its betting
exchange? No, it did not. It didn't need to, because all
the relevant information was in Andrew Black's head.
He knew what big punters wanted and that they weren't
getting it. He designed the betting exchange to provide
the missing ingredients.

Why, then, have I made such a fuss about comb charts? Because they provide an extremely useful way of thinking about the customers you propose to target and the benefits your new category will provide relative to the main market.

To launch a star venture successfully, three conditions *must* apply.

1. Your target customers want something different from the main market.

2. You understand what it is that they want and can provide it with a new product category.

3. The new category can be supplied profitably, because you can charge more for it, and/or because you can subtract elements of the main market product that are expensive to provide, so that the new category has lower costs than the main market.

The best way to check on conditions 1 and 2 is to draw a chart similar to Figure 10.4. You don't need hard data to do this. Start out with a view about the target customers and what they are not getting but would like. Then think how the new category could provide the missing wants. When you have a clear picture, talk to some target customers to confirm or modify your assumptions.

Alternatively, work backwards from thinking what you could supply that is different from the main market, and then think which target customers would be ideal for the new category. Such 'backward' thinking − fitting the market to the product − is disapproved of by most marketing experts but in practice the world often works this way. Who knew ahead of time that Americans would like Honda's scooters? Nobody at Honda. Who knew that secretaries and executives would love Post-it Notes? Nobody at 3M. Who knew that a computer would eventually sit on most office desks? Nobody at IBM.

The great thing about Figure 10.4 is that you can play around with a large number of potential markets, new categories and customer groups until you get a picture like the one for betting exchanges. *Then* you can be confident that the idea will work.

Step 5: Ensure profitable variation

Do the potential niches on your shortlist promise profitable variation? Figure 10.5 shows the two ways that profitable variation can occur. In new niche 'A' the price

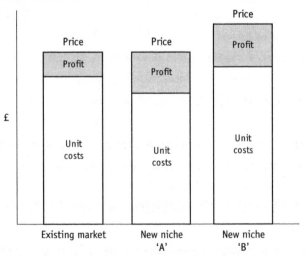

Figure 10.5 Profitable variation

and value are the same as in the main market, but the unit costs are lower for the new niche and the profit therefore higher. New niche 'B' shows the other route to profitable variation – the same costs as the main market, but higher value delivered to customers and therefore a higher price.

A new niche is worth creating only if it will be more profitable than the existing market.

Step 6: Name the new niche

Can you think of a good name for the new niches on your shortlist (not for your brand, but for the *category* you are creating)? If you can't, that may indicate some confusion about the real advantages of the niche and its difference from the main market.

A good niche name

★ is short;

★ is easy to understand;

★ describes the niche;

★ is unique – it does not duplicate any other niche description, and could not be confused with another one; and

★ will be used by all competitors to describe the niche.

'Betting exchange', 'personal organiser', 'hamburger restaurant', 'modern circus', 'cola drink', 'convenience store', 'light beer', 'energy drink', 'play analyser' all qualify.

Competing names for the same new category – 'electronic organiser', 'personal digital assistant (PDA)', 'handheld computer' – are a sure sign of sloppy thinking.

Step 7: Name the new brand

If you are clear and confident about the new niche, its high growth, target market and benefits, and why the variation is profitable, then it's not essential to decide the new brand name right now. If you can, great. If you're trying to decide between two equally attractive new star ventures, and can think of a great brand name in one case but not the other, that may just tip the balance in your decision.

Make the name

★ very short (two syllables or preferably one);

★ sound nice;

★ punchy;

★ memorable;

★ easy to say;

★ unique and original (not similar to any other brand);

★ resonate with the niche.

brand	short	sounds nice	punchy	mem- orable	easy to say	unique	reso- nates with niche
Red Bull	yes	yes	yes	yes	yes	yes	yes
Quicken	yes	yes	yes	yes	yes	yes	yes
Intel	yes	yes	yes	yes	yes	yes	yes
Belgo	yes	yes	yes	yes	yes	yes	yes
Betfair	yes	yes	yes	yes	yes	yes	yes
Filofax	yes	yes	yes	yes	yes	yes	yes
Coca-Cola (Coke)	yes	yes	yes	yes	yes	yes	yes
7-11	yes	yes	yes	yes	yes	yes	yes
Toys 'R' Us	yes	yes	yes	yes	yes	yes	yes
McDonald's	yes	yes	yes	yes	yes	yes	yes
Jeep	yes	yes	yes	yes	yes	yes	yes
Ford	yes	yes	yes	yes	yes	yes	no
Starbucks	yes	yes	yes	yes	yes	yes	no
Nokia	yes	yes	yes	yes	yes	yes	no
Rolex	yes	yes	yes	yes	yes	yes	no
Flutter	yes	yes	no	yes	yes	yes	no
Wal-Mart	yes	no	no	no	yes	yes	no
KMX[1]	yes	no	no	no	yes	yes	no
Duryea [2]	yes	no	no	no	no	yes	no
Gablin- ger's [3]	no	no	no	no	no	yes	no
Motorola Dyna TAC 8000 [4]	no	no	no	no	no	no	no

Figure 10.6 Brand name evaluator

[1] Coca-Cola's unsuccessful rival to Red Bull. [2] Duryea was America's first automobile brand. [3] Gablinger's was the first light beer. [4] The first cellphone, introduced in 1983. Source: Loosely based on Al and Laura Ries (2004) *The Origin of Brands* (New York: HarperCollins).

Now make your own shortlist of brand names, similar to figure 10.6, above, and evaluate your suggestions with ticks and crosses.

Ranking of your star venture shortlist

Now is the time we've all been waiting for! If you're not sure which star venture idea to go for by now, summarise the appeal of each shortlisted idea under the steps we've examined:

Shortlisted Ideas	Likely Niche Growth Rate	Clear Target Customers	Benefits of Niche	Profitable Variation	Good Niche Name	Good Brand

Ranking of Opportunity

(1)

(2)

(3)

Allocate one to three ticks for each idea under the six evaluation headings. Then decide your overall ranking of possible star ventures.

Figure 10.7 Final evaluation of your shortlist
of possible star ventures

Do you have your idea now? Go and toast your coming millions! This is precisely what my friends André and Denis did, after we had agreed that Belgo would become a star venture, before they began building it. Some would call it 'hubris'. I call it 'justified confidence in the power of the star idea'. If the idea meets the rules we've gone through, there will be a way of making it work. If you're not sure about the idea, wait until you find something that has you brimming with confidence. Save your energy for the best idea you can find, one where you're excited and certain.

11

Benefit from
somebody else's star

The secret to creativity is knowing how to hide your sources.
Albert Einstein

This is a short chapter, but brevity is the soul of wealth. Here you will learn how to ride a star already created, and become hugely successful with relatively little effort.

You don't have to start a star venture to enjoy its benefits. It's much easier to piggyback on someone else's idea and hard graft. Arguably, the ratio of reward to effort is much higher if you spot a star – early enough – rather than start one.

The wonderful thing about spotting a star is that it can be quite easy – provided you know what you are looking for. I did not invest in Betfair when it started, but a few months later, when it was already growing fast. To me it was obviously a star, and I put as much money in as they would let me. So far I have received a return of 53 times my original investment, and more money than all my other gains put together. I benefited from somebody else's star. They had the idea. They raised the cash. They launched the business. They proved the concept in practice. They generated enormous growth. They sowed and they reaped mightily. But I reaped mightily too.

So can you. You don't even have to be an investor, but, if you can put any spare cash into a star, that will probably be wise. Most of us work for a living. Why not work for a baby star venture? There are two huge advantages.

The first is *fun*. As one of the early employees, you'll be important. You'll have a hand in making the business a success. You'll feel part of the venture, and it will feel part of you. I promise you, nothing is more fun. Yes, it will sometimes be frustrating. Yes, you will work hard. Yes, it will intrude on your private life. Yes, it will test the limits of your abilities. Yes, it will be intense. But you'll be engaged. You'll be fascinated. You'll never be bored.

You'll make some of the most important, intense and long-lasting friendships of your life. If you're unattached, there's a good chance you'll meet your partner in the venture and you'll know their essential character before you commit to them (don't ask me why so many great relationships start in star ventures, I just know that they do). You won't feel that you're working for someone else, but for a great shared endeavour with your colleagues. In short, you will *live*. You'll pulsate with energy. You'll be attractive and fulfilled.

Then there's *money*. Almost certainly, if you are astute, you will make far more money out of a star than from a normal job. True, right at the start, you may not be paid as much. Small ventures usually pay less for the same type of person. Before long, however, as the star begins to do very well, pay and benefits are likely to become very generous – don't get me started on Betfair, where all employees have *six weeks' annual holiday* and were paid extremely well, as soon as the firm broke even and started to gush cash. The real payoff, though, comes from stock options and the ability to buy shares in the company. Most baby firms give their early employees options. You don't have to pay for these until they are valuable, so you can make real money without taking any risk.

There *are* disadvantages. You shouldn't join a star venture if you are lazy, a loner, in poor health, don't want to be committed, tired of life or in a relationship that is already shaky – it would not survive the competition! Otherwise, it's a 'no-brainer'.

If you have normal ambition and interest in work, you will be much happier and wealthier if you join a baby business that is already a star. The issue is not *whether* to work in a star, but rather *how* to find one.

What are you looking for? A baby business. Something young and small – under 20 employees if you are looking for a job; and something too small or unproven to attract professional investment if you are an investor.

★ **A baby business growing very fast.** Any small business growing *very* fast is *likely* to be a star. Every star business *will* be growing fast. So growth is a good first screen of any baby business you find.

★ **An original idea.** A baby business that has found a gap in the market – the creator of a new way of doing business. A star venture will be doing things differently.

★ **Baby is a leader.** In its gap, in its own business arena, it is the largest. It may have one or two even younger imitators, but most likely it is still unique.

★ **Baby's customers are different.** You can see why the baby business appeals to particular customers, who can't get anything as attractive to them elsewhere.

★ **A baby business that you can imagine being extremely profitable when it grows up.** There must be hard economic reasons why the business, when it reaches the size it can, will have fat margins. Its costs must be much lower than the conventional way of doing business, or its prices must be higher, or both.

How to find your star

★ **Make it front of mind every day.** When you get up, say to yourself, 'Today I'm going to look for my star.' If you make to-do lists, put it at the top.

★ **Keep your eyes and ears open.** Every moment of the day, be looking for your star. Once you consciously search for stars, it's amazing how they turn up.

★ **Put up a sign.** At work, at home, put up a sign that says FIND MY STAR. Place the sign where other people will see it and ask you what it means. Get them looking on your behalf. (If your boss asks, tell him or her that you're looking for a great new idea or friend. This is true and it won't get you into trouble.)

★ **Look at websites.** The Web takes us on magical mystery tours. As you navigate sites of small firms, think, 'Does this have the hallmarks of a star venture?'

★ **Ask your friends.** Every time you see or call a friend you haven't met for a while, ask them if they know of a new business 'like this . . .'

★ **Form a Star Alliance** with two or three friends, dedicated to finding a star. Choose people you really trust, who also want to find a star. Meet often to track progress.

What to do next

What do you do when you've found a baby business you think may be a star?

★ **Talk to them.** Find a reason to talk to everyone in and around the company, to express your interest and learn more.

★ **Do them a favour.** If you can, buy something from them. Point them towards other customers. Advise them on how to expand.

★ **Discreetly verify that it is a star.** Ask questions suggested in the section above, 'What are you looking for?'

★ **Work out a job you could do for them.** Don't wait for them to post a vacancy. Tell them what you can do, why they should hire you. Stress the benefits you bring.

★ **Make your mark.** When you join the firm, work out *one thing* you can do within your first month that will visibly benefit your colleagues and the venture.

★ **Check again from the inside that it really is a star.** If the business isn't really growing very fast, or doesn't fit the bill in any other way, don't hang around. If it really is a star, work out how far the star could rise.

★ **Raise ambition within the firm.** Sometimes the founders of a star don't see its potential. Open their eyes. Tell them how valuable the firm could become, if expanded to its maximum potential. Consider whether the idea can be exported to other countries, and/or franchised. Would other channels of distribution (such as the phone with Betfair) enlarge the market?

★ **Consider making an offer for the firm.** If the founders really don't 'get it', put together a group to buy the firm. Remember the astronomical return Ray Kroc achieved from buying McDonald's from the founders, when it was already highly successful.

Conclusion

It won't take you too long to find your star. Nor is it difficult. It just takes determination, application and energy.

The benefits are out of all proportion to the effort. Forgive the snake-oil cliché, but in this case it's true — when you've found your star, your life will never be the same again.

I've derived enormous gratification, enjoyment and financial gain from working and investing in my five star ventures. Each chapter of my life since I was 30 has been framed by one of them. I hope that you, too, having tasted the delights of one star, will go on to become a serial star venturer. Maybe you'll enjoy working in star after star and build a great reputation as an entrepreneur. Or maybe, having worked in one star and made money from it, you'll want to take life easier. You can still invest in other stars and share their thrills, rewards and glory without having to work in them.

12

Fake stars

Run from disaster rather than be caught by it.
Homer (The Iliad)

Mark Allin and Richard Burton started Capstone, their book-publishing venture, with high hopes. False modesty aside, they knew they were excellent editors, with a great track record at two publishing giants. I could vouch for Mark Allin's profit-making abilities, since he gave me the idea for writing *The 80/20 Principle*, my bestselling book. Richard and Mark envisaged Capstone as a star venture, the leader in a new category of '*funky* business books'. They convinced me that this idea was plausible and I became their financial backer. I reckoned that I had an 'each-way bet' – either their star business would materialise, or, at worst, they would pick a few great winners, making Capstone highly profitable.

The business appeared to start well. They commissioned a stream of trendy books from interesting authors. The product looked great, with distinctive trendy designs. Mark and Richard were full of ideas and enthusiasm, confidently projecting sales that would give us good profits.

The only thing was, the forecasts never materialised.

Whenever we looked at the numbers we were constantly disappointed. I kept injecting cash, and it kept vanishing. To this day I don't know why their books didn't sell in quantities we could reasonably expect. The favoured explanation was the weakness of the sales force – inevitably, it was difficult to acquire distribution muscle from scratch. Maybe they just had bad luck in not commissioning any smash hits. Whatever the reason, Capstone was a financial black hole.

I remember a rather difficult meeting at my home in Richmond some three years after the start. Richard and Mark asked for a further loan to commission new books. I had to say no. We had to face facts. Capstone was not a star; the category of 'funky business books' had not established itself. Capstone was a rather weak follower in the business-books arena. Capstone had none of the financial attributes of a star. If it looked like a dog, behaved like a dog and barked like a dog, it probably was a dog.

Could we change our ambitions for Capstone, and make it into a star by championing a new category? We thought hard and long, but couldn't come up with a convincing idea.

We asked Robin Field, who had done a great job running Filofax, to become Capstone's interim chairman. Robin confirmed our diagnosis. We should do two things, he said. One, conserve cash as much as possible, cutting working capital and publishing fewer books. Two, sell the business.

At least we had something to sell. Although it was not a star business, Richard and Mark had created a brand with resonance and value. Certainly one big international publisher thought so – we sold Capstone to John Wiley. Capstone still lives on as part of the Wiley stable. I recovered all of my loans and interest and made nearly nine times return on my equity. Mark and Richard did well out of the sale, and continued to run Capstone happily for its new owners.

Richard has since left to start another business, Infinite Ideas, which looks like a real star venture. Infinite Ideas has created a unique, profitable, fast-growth segment, publishing practical, 'how to' ideas to improve lives, on subjects such as *Beat Back Pain* or *Healthy Cooking for Children*. The book content is then recycled through deals with relevant companies. For example, 60,000 copies of a short *Detox* book have been put on packs of Tetley decaffeinated tea; and a *Secrets of Wine* book has been followed by a book specially adapted for the wine touring company Grape Escapes. Infinite Ideas keeps exclusive copyright to its content and is thus free to republish it at high margins.

Though not a financial disaster, the Capstone story is salutary. It shows how easy it is to be over-optimistic. It shows the importance of watching cash flow, and having a financial person as part of the top team (we never did). It shows that starting a new venture, even with great executives, can turn out to be more difficult than anyone imagined. It shows that selling a young business (without star potential) can be infinitely preferable to throwing more cash at it. It also shows that running a non-star venture can be a great education and prelude to a much better entrepreneurial experience.

But the lesson I want to focus on in this chapter is simply this: not all ventures that aim to be stars turn out to be stars. How do you diagnose a fake star? What do you do when your 'star' fails to take off?

The star principle

Anatomy of the fake star

The business definition does not establish itself – the new category (such as 'funky business books') is not a viable niche. There may have been a gap in the market, but there wasn't a profitable market in the gap.

There is no shame in this. You find out only by putting the idea out into the market. Who knows at the start? There have been many wonderful ideas and inventions that never found a big enough market to make money. Who could have been sure, before the event, that Belgo's funky restaurants would work and Capstone's funky books would not? I don't have this expertise and don't know anyone who does.

Fake stars may be impossible to spot at the outset. But, once a venture has been running for a little time, it's easy to tell.

★ The new category doesn't turn out to be sufficiently different from the main market.

★ It hasn't built a cadre of enthusiastic customers who are identifiably different from the main market.

★ It isn't growing very fast. Typically the fake star has no imitators, and the fake star itself, after an initial burst, doesn't grow each month.

★ It isn't very profitable. OK, no business is going to be profitable on day one. But the projected break-even of the fake star keeps receding. If you extrapolate the sales growth of the fake star, it will never break even. The costs of the fake star are not lower than those in the main market and its prices are not higher.

What if you're employed in a fake star?

Immediately you realise that your 'star' is really a question mark or a dog in drag, think whether the firm can be evolved into a star (see Chapter 14).

Convince the founders that the current strategy isn't working. Try to develop a new route to stardom.

If the founders won't listen, or the attempt doesn't work, look for a job in a real star. You will feel the pull of loyalty to colleagues. Disengaging is always messy, but your energies will be more useful and effective in a real star. What's wrong with talent gravitating to where it can do most good?

What if you've invested in a fake star?

Try very hard to evolve the venture into a real star. Right now, the fake star has little value. If you can find a new niche to dominate – one that really takes off and grows – it will make you rich.

But be realistic. If you can't imagine a viable new category suitable for the venture, or if you try, and fail again, there's only one answer: sell the business while you can, while it still appears to have unfulfilled potential. Since the business can't perform, sell it on hope.

Happily, most potential buyers don't think in terms of stars, fake stars and non-stars. A bigger rival may see your fake star as a nice little venture that can be greatly improved through access to the buyer's strong points (maybe its market muscle, its sales force, its R&D, its manufacturing). Wiley thought its sales force could sell many more copies of Capstone books than an independent Capstone could, and that it could slash Capstone's admin costs. All you can do is hope potential buyers believe in synergy. If they do, take the money and run.

If the fake star can't be sold, run it for cash. Don't put any more cash in – it will get trapped and never escape (hence the phrase 'cash trap'). Take cash out, even if this dooms the venture.

Use your cash for real stars, not to prop up ailing fake stars.

Non-stars

A 'non-star' is not usually a fake star, but simply one of the other positions on the BCG matrix – a dog, question mark or cash cow.

The *cash cow* is a leader in its category but the category is not growing fast. Since 1993 I have owned a hotel venture, now called Zola Hotels, that's a cash cow. It has a viable and unique niche based around the skills of the two hoteliers who run it. Zola takes over badly run hotels that are the biggest in their category locally, builds new bedrooms and then sells the hotels again. Zola is a nice, profitable venture – my cash invested in Zola has gone up four times.

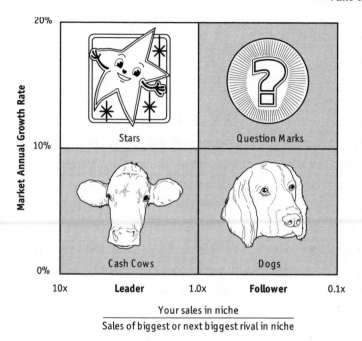

Figure 12.1 Relative market share

But the market is relatively small and constrained by the time of its two leaders.

If you own a cash cow you usually make a good living, but probably won't become really rich. The most that employees can hope for is a comfortable existence.

A *question mark* operates in a fast-growth market, but is not the leader. The value of a question-mark venture depends on its prospects for overtaking the leader. If it is a weak question mark, as Capstone was, the chances may be virtually nil. Yet, if the question mark is not too far behind the leader and gaining fast, it may turn into a star. If it doesn't, investors and employees alike are wasting their time.

To mix zoological metaphors, the real albatross is the *dog*. It's of no value to employees or investors!

Conclusion

Not every new category idea – not every potential star business – works as well in practice as in theory. When you have a star that isn't working, it's nearly always a fake star. Whether you're an owner or employee, face the truth. Evolve into a star if you can, by doing something radically different. Failing that, sell out or get out.

Energy should flow into real stars. There are only two real blunders that entrepreneurs make. One is to persevere with losing causes. The other, far graver, error is not to realise the marvellously rich potential of a star venture.

part three
nurture a star

13

The star takes off

The manager is a hero in the West, but an imposter. The concept of management has proved a huge distraction. The management side of running a company is trivial compared to the importance of being commercial or entrepreneurial, or having a particular specialist skill. Any organization needs to have people with the skills relevant to its business, rather than turning people into general managers.

Andrew Campbell

O nce you have started a star venture, there is one more critical step before you have a valuable business – the take-off. To make the business take off, you and your colleagues need to *translate* the star idea into a *business formula that works in practice* and that can be expanded indefinitely. The take-off is typically a messy process of trial and error, two steps forward and one step back, when *everyone* in the firm can lend a hand and sometimes the most valuable moves are made by accident and by quite junior people.

In the take-off we see the *many-headed entrepreneur* at work, the founders and the first 20 employees all pitching in to try to get the venture rolling down the runway and into the skies. Every successful venture then looks back with mingled pride and wonder on the pratfalls, improvised genius, breakthroughs and near-disasters that defined the character of the firm: the late nights and early mornings; the improvisations and scheming to get a hearing from a big buyer; the trip to persuade him to give the firm a go; the frenzy to prepare the pitch or the first products for that customer; the bloody-minded determination to deliver a great product against the clock, against the odds, and against the undeniable fact that nobody really knew what they were doing, because nobody had done it before. All great fun and the stuff of nostalgic war stories, unless it drove you to drink or nervous breakdown.

Through the chaos and variety of different start-ups, we can glimpse a pattern that is the same in all successful take-offs. Knowing the pattern will enable you to avoid some – though not all – of the frustrations and false turns to which every baby business is prey. In every star venture I have known, there were in retrospect *four formulas* that had to be discovered and turned into routine, unique and consistently repeatable business practices:

1. **the customer-attraction formula:** the way to get an ever-increasing number of profitable customers who buy more and more from you;

2. **the commercial formula:** the way to lock in fat margins;

3. **the delivery formula:** the way to forge a machine delivering ever-increasing quantities of consistent and high-quality product; and

4. **the innovation formula**: the way to make innovation and improvement routine, to keep clear of rivals.

The formulas have to fit together and have 'integrity' – wholeness, sincerity, consistency, coherence and authenticity – so that each formula is not only consistent with the other three, but also reinforces them. For your venture to be a star, the formulas must be *unique* and *better* – better than any formula in the main market, and better than any competing formula in the new category you have created. To remain a star, the formulas must be capable of infinite extension and deepening, so that rivals cannot fully understand them, imitate them or replace them with better formulas. Ultimately, 'better' is not a matter of opinion. It is a matter of votes, customers' votes in the marketplace. A 'better' formula is one that is more profitable and achieves higher market share and faster growth than any rival formula.

1: The customer-attraction formula

This formula is a *reliable way of getting ever-increasing volumes of profitable business*. The customer-attraction formula has two parts:

★ the *difference* about the new product and category that is *attractive* to the *target customers*; and

★ an organised process of PR and selling that enables sales to take off, so that there is a *consistent and attractive message* going to customers and potential customers, resulting in *prolonged sales growth*; until there is consistent sales growth above 10 per cent a year (and ideally *much* higher in the early years), take-off is not secure.

The starting point is always the product itself. *That* has to be different, attractive, appealing. It has to offer something, in some way, that the main market does not. If the work in designing the new product, category and brand has been done well, then there should be no problem about its *difference* and value to target customers:

★ Betfair: hugely greater value

★ Coke: unique refreshing taste, the real thing

★ Filofax: *personal* organisation

★ Plymouth Gin: sophisticated and different taste, higher strength

★ Bain & Company: Bain–CEO relationship

★ Belgo: Belgian food, beer and fun

★ Starbucks: exotic authentic coffee

★ McDonald's: fast, cheap hamburgers

★ Quicken: manage your finances easily

★ Dell: PC tailored for you

The customer-attraction formula takes a magnetic product and exposes it in such a way that business materialises and grows. No customer-attraction formula, however brilliant, can ever make a star out of something earthbound. On the other hand, a product such as Betfair, which gave customers 10 or 20 times better value, spread like wildfire.

The message going to potential Betfair users was quite simply the extraordinary *value* offered, a true *revolution* in betting. The value proposition was reinforced by all kinds of secondary themes, above all the delight in bypassing the hated bookmakers.

Yet Betfair would not have taken off without masses of PR. Andrew Black and Mark Davies, a junior employee with no training in PR but who demonstrated immense aptitude for it, spent most of their time in the first three years talking to racing journalists, generating a fantastic amount of free press, radio and TV coverage. We gave Mark a business card saying 'managing director', though at first the only person he managed was himself.

Slowly but surely the message got home to almost every serious gambler in the UK. Betfair's growth was initially fuelled by a small number of big betters who were also nerds and techno-freaks. The growth could not have been sustained without of tens of thousands of big gamblers who were not technophiles and would never have heard of betting exchanges had they not been featured every day in the *Racing Post* and on Channel 4 TV, a direct result of work by Andrew and Mark. It was to the immense credit of Ed Wray, Betfair's CEO, that he stood aside and gave every chance to appear on TV to Mark Davies, whose good looks, intimate knowledge of racing, quick wit and upper-class charm quickly made him a favourite with TV editors and producers.

In nearly every star take-off that I know intimately or have researched, the customer-attraction formula was based heavily on public relations and word of mouth. PR launched stars such as Belgo, Filofax, Betfair, Coca-Cola, Cirque du Soleil, Starbucks and Curves. Once PR had induced a few customers to try the new product, word of mouth brought a cascade of customers. PR then re-inforced and multiplied that momentum. For the first two years after the first Belgo restaurant was opened, the two founders spent more than half their time on PR-related activities. We couldn't afford any advertising, and it would have been a waste of money, anyway. But you listen to your friends, to independent food critics, and to journal-ists who say a nice place is fun. André and Denis worked creatively and tirelessly to get the volume of noise about Belgo to levels where it could be heard above the loud background hum of London life.

Some people are naturals at PR. Others don't have the gift of catching the attention of busy, flighty media folk. Some are good at the set-piece speech but not at small talk. If you have one or two employees who might be good at PR, give them a chance to shine. Seniority doesn't matter at all. If you really don't have anyone gifted at PR, you must hire someone; but an ounce of empathy with the product and customers is worth a ton of general PR experience.

Many people think that word of mouth and PR are automatic processes, that the firm sits back and enjoys a stream of free publicity. Rubbish! PR requires capturing the imagination of jaded journalists. To do so you must *craft a general storyline* and then *adapt it to the individual journalist.*

At Plymouth Gin we carefully distilled not just our product but also its heritage – all the guff about the distillery being a former Franciscan monastery, the place where the Pilgrim Fathers stayed en route to the New World, the oldest gin distillery in the world, and so on. *Anything* to generate column inches in the most prestigious papers and airtime on food and drink programmes. You might have thought we were selling the Ark of the Covenant or the Holy Grail rather than intoxicating liquor!

Image is vital. The past pervades the present. The past has to be created. The message for Plymouth Gin's potential customers was clear: this is a *different, sophisticated gin, with a history no other gin can match.* But the difference had to be more than assertion and a rose-tinted reconstruction of history. For the PR to bite, there had to be an *objective difference* that would lend credibility to the 'colour' that we gave the brand. We found that difference by making Plymouth a higher-strength gin at a time when Gordon's, the market leader in the main market, was moving the other way, reducing its strength. Putting the alcohol in Plymouth Gin up to 41.2 per cent had a real consumer benefit, because the increased strength greatly enhanced Plymouth's distinctive taste – the reason why the gin had been the market leader in the first quarter of the twentieth century. The PR worked because nobody could deny that Plymouth was high strength and because gin aficionados vouched for the superior taste.

Word of mouth may sound a gift from the gods, but no!

The star principle

It has to be manufactured and amplified, and it has to rest on a real consumer benefit. As the *New Yorker* columnist and bestselling author Malcolm Gladwell has shown, word of mouth can flare up and quickly die or it can reach the 'tipping point' where no force on earth can arrest the product's relentless forward march. The art of the entrepreneur is to get word of mouth to the tipping point.

Bain & Company, the American strategy consulting firm, had a clear, attractive message to its target market of CEOs (especially new CEOs from outside the company):

> We will help turbo-charge the value of the company. We will be your faithful allies and loyal to you. We will help you make sense of the new world you have entered, and give you intelligence about what is going on in every nook and cranny of your firm. We will give you every piece of information and analysis you need to take tough decisions and make huge changes. We will work only for you, never for your competitors.

Although the message was original and attractive, the tough thing in the early days, outside the US, was getting a hearing. Once we had a hearing, the thing that stopped CEOs buying a very expensive service from us was that we were unknown. Our firm had no reputation in Europe.

When I was an early employee of Bain in London, every top executive had heard of McKinsey but nobody outside the industry had heard of Bain & Company. When we met a chief executive prospect, we encouraged him to visit our well-known competitors and pose one specific question. The CEO would be invited to ask, say, the

180

McKinsey partner he saw this question: 'If, for any reason, your firm could not work with us, which other strategy consultant should I consider employing?' Invariably, the partner would respond along the lines, 'BCG or Bain & Company', since these were indeed his firm's top rivals in the United States. Many of the CEOs who became our first Bain & Company clients in London told us they came largely because of this recommendation from our rivals — it enabled our future clients to place an unknown firm in the same bracket as the world's most prestigious firms. Yet we fabricated the 'word of mouth'; we encouraged the CEOs to ask the right question.

Bain honed their customer-attraction formula to perfection:

★ identify newly appointed chief executives of large companies;

★ research the companies and work out how to turbo-charge the firm's value;

★ procure a meeting with the CEO;

★ use the research to coax the CEO to open up on how he saw his new company;

★ the Bain partners would lay out the Bain contract between the CEO and Bain;

★ get a Bain client who knew the CEO to say how wonderful we were;

★ most important of all, when appointed, find more and
more work where Bain could add increased value (and
greatly increased Bain billings) to the client organisation.

You know that you have crossed the first hurdle to take-
off when sales growth is no longer a problem. You still
have three hurdles to jump.

2: The commercial formula

If your thinking on 'profitable variation' (Step 5 of the
Seven Steps to Heaven) has been good enough, it may
translate easily into the commercial formula. But it can be
one thing to sit down with a glass of wine and work out
why your new star business can be more profitable than
the main market, and quite another to encounter your
bookkeeper after a few months and learn whether you
really are on track for profitable variation.

At Belgo, we had reckoned that the menu, heavily
weighted towards mussels and *frites* and Belgian monastery beer, would produce a gross margin of around 70 per
cent (for every 100 pence of food or drink we sold, it cost
us only 30 pence). On that basis, with revenue building
every day, we were soon able to cover our fixed costs and
start to generate a nice flow of cash. Of course there were
crises. Our biggest problem was getting a sufficient supply
of large, high-quality mussels. We soon became Britain's largest purchaser of mussels and our ever-increasing
demand drove prices up.

One morning the Belgo 'boys' (André and Denis) came

to me with long faces and furrowed brows. There was a sudden shortage of mussels. Overnight, the price had spurted 20p a kilo. Gross margins would plummet below 70 per cent. What were we to do?

'Put the price up by a pound,' I said.

'That would kill demand,' André replied.

'Well, let's try it for one day, and, if that works, another day, and, if demand doesn't dip, we'll keep the price there,' I said. 'If people switch to another menu item or stop coming we can always lower the price again. And, while we're printing new menus, let's hoist the prices of our three top beers.'

They didn't like it. But the price hikes made absolutely no difference to how much beer and mussels we sold. Despite the higher mussels cost, our gross margin inched up to 72–3 per cent, the highest in the industry. Within 18 months of opening we were able to convert the next-door space, double capacity and start repaying shareholder loans.

At Betfair, too, the original concept featured such strong profitable variation (versus the traditional bookmaker market) that the commercial formula required little further elaboration. A few months after I made my investment, it became clear that, if volumes continued growing strongly, the business would soon become highly profitable and cash-positive.

Plymouth Gin's 'profitable variation' required us to believe that we could charge a very high price for the gin (similar to other 'super-premium' gins), while having much lower overheads and no advertising costs. The high price proved possible, but in the first three years we failed to get enough PR to generate substantial consumer demand and get listings in major stores. Then we hit gold with our third chief executive, Charles Rolls, and his decision to raise our gin strength.

For Filofax, 'profitable variation' always meant a high utility for the personal-organiser user relative to a diary or pad of paper. Result: fat margins.

When we started LEK we didn't know about 'profitable variation'. We knew strategy consulting was very profitable – given a constant stream of clients. We didn't have that, either.

We were saved by our incompetence at recruiting MBA consultants, and by our success in hiring 21-year-old graduates. We had masses of very smart young men and women who knew nothing about business. We dared not send them to clients. What could they do? We gave them all personal computers – generous and daring, we thought – and trained them to analyse clients' competitors, through financial and market analysis and talking in the marketplace.

Why would any client want competitor analysis? Well, as with Microfile versus Filofax, it might point to opportunities to gain market share or cut costs. We devised a new product called *relative cost position*. By looking at the costs of the client and rivals at every stage (product cost, manufacturing, marketing, selling, distribution, all overheads), we could find practical ways to reduce costs, when the competitor had lower costs, or to raise prices, when the competitor's costs were higher. We sold our relative-cost-position product to all our clients. They loved it. That gave us confidence to sell to new clients.

What had happened? We had a problem, a glut of inexperienced analysts. We found something they could do well. We discovered a great product. We sold it. All trial and error.

And very profitable for LEK. The 'kids' were cheap. They worked long hours with no payment for overtime. We charged a lot for their work. Competitors didn't have our bottom-heavy staff structure, so couldn't imitate us economically.

Later we focused on mergers-and-acquisitions investigation and analysis, another product ideally suited to our bottom-heavy staff structure. Upshot: high prices, low costs, fat margins, fast growth. Profitable variation.

3. The delivery formula

OK, customer demand and margins are high. What next? Deliver the product. Make things happen reliably, consistently, economically. Make the venture a *machine*.

Early on, what matters is winning orders, and pushing product out of the door any which way. But take-off requires a sturdy production engine. A machine that operates to meticulous standards and does everything *one* way, the way that assures efficiency *and* quality.

Typically, founders aren't very interested in 'the firm as machine'. Too bad. Without the lowest possible cost, and the highest possible quality and consistency, the business is exposed to one certainty and one danger.

The certainty is that you will be less profitable than you could be, so whatever you eventually realise for the business will be 25–50 per cent less than it could be. The danger is that sloppy operating lets a better-organised rival get within reach of you, as happened with Filofax and Microfile.

Thank goodness there is usually someone around to organise the new firm, given half a chance! At Betfair it was an ex-army chap called Jon Cumberledge. At LEK it was my former secretary, a great lady called Jeanette Shand; 20 years later, she is still there. At Filofax it was my partner Robin Field. At Plymouth Gin, it was the distillery manager, Sean Harrison. At Belgo, it was founder André Plisnier. In all cases they were assisted by several other people, the many-headed entrepreneur taking care of business.

The delivery formula has been cracked when *all* the following events *always* happen.

★ Products are delivered to the same high standard, on time, every time.

★ This year's product is measurably better than last year's.

★ This year's product costs at least 5 per cent less to make than last year's.

★ Volumes can be doubled within a year without panic or loss of quality.

★ Work is delegated to the lowest-level person who is fully competent to do it.

★ Everyone increases his or her skill level significantly each year and works better and faster.

★ The workplace exudes calm, order and discipline.

★ Standards and procedures are written down, clear, unambiguous – and observed!

★ Logos, colours and designs are attractive and consistent.

★ Budgets are always met or exceeded.

★ Cash is always higher than planned.

★ The firm is a machine – smooth-running, reliable, relentless, self-maintaining and self-improving.

★ Nobody is indispensable. If the best people leave, the firm rolls on regardless. New leaders come to the fore.

This may not be your idea of an entrepreneurial venture. Yet every star venture that takes off and stays high is a robust flying machine. It has order and organisation. It keeps its promises to customers, employees and owners.

Stars create their niches. But, if they are not perfectly aligned to serve them efficiently, somebody else will. The old star burns up.

4. The innovation formula

How do the best stars innovate? They don't move into yet another category, or do anything at odds with their original blueprint. Innovation in the most successful stars means moving further and further, higher and deeper, wider and stronger, in the direction you pioneered in the first place. Innovation increases the difference between stars and rivals, making the stars uniquely fitted to serve their target customers. The megastars closely penetrate their customers' desires in the chosen category, becoming a key part of their daily life and sometimes even their self-identity. The stars widen the gulf between their capabilities in your niche and any other firm's. The stars delight in giving customers pleasant surprises, making a switch to another supplier unthinkable. Stars become irreplaceable. Change is the means to ensure that there cannot be any change in market leadership.

Analysis of valuable stars reveals three golden rules of innovation.

1. Innovation is best *based on what you already do best* and most *distinctively*. Innovation is powerful when it suits the *new category* you have invented rather than the main market, because it makes the new category even more attractive to its target customers.

2. Effective innovation *makes it impossible for competitors to catch up*. This type of innovation never stops. Rivals can't get closer because the stars are always widening the gap in value delivered to customers.

3. The best innovation *reinforces and extends profitable variation*. Innovation is not charity. Real, sustainable innovation kills two birds with one stone – it makes customers happier, and it make your venture more profitable.

Innovation is hard. It takes deviant thinking and persistent non-routine action. *There is no point, therefore, in wasting precious energy on innovation that does not satisfy all three golden rules.*

The decision to pursue a major innovation is fateful. Bad innovation drives out good.

When we asked Belgo's core customers what they liked best, we thought they would highlight the food and the service. Though these scored well, the things about Belgo they loved most were the monastery beers and the unique ambience: the sophisticated, Continental European jollity of the place. Belgo's first major innovation, therefore, was to introduce the Bierodrome, a new chain of 'mini-Belgo' outlets with the accent on the beer. Bar space outranked eating space, providing a full selection of our beers and a cut-down menu. Customers flocked to the Bierodromes. They also extended Belgo's profitable variation. It is a great deal easier to open a bottle of beer than to cook a meal, and the return on capital is a lot higher. The Bierodrome also made it more difficult for competitors to catch up, now that there were two related concepts rather than one.

Less than a year after it started, Betfair introduced two important 'golden rule' innovations. One was betting in-play – customers could bet while an event (a race, a soccer or tennis match, a golf tournament, an election) was going on.

★ In-play betting, particularly on a fast-changing event such as a horse race, was ideally suited to an electronic market where the odds are set automatically and instantly by supply and demand. The main world of betting – with bookmakers setting the odds – is a one-way market, where the bookmakers set the odds and punters take them or leave them. A one-way market responds too slowly to shifts in fortune in a volatile event. More than five years after Betfair introduced in-play horserace betting, no traditional bookmaker has been able to offer the service.

★ The attraction of betting in-play is particularly great for the target customers – big, sophisticated gamblers. Betting while an event is going on requires sharp eyes and strong nerves. It's a great test of skill. It also enables big gamblers to 'lay off' their positions during an event or to lock in a profit. By pioneering in-play, Betfair gained by far the largest liquidity in this area. No other betting exchange has come anywhere close.

★ In-play extends profitable variation. Betfair can extract more revenue and more commission from the same event.

I suggested the other innovation shortly after I invested. At the time Betfair and other betting exchanges offered only online betting. Why not use the telephone as well?

Telephone bets could be fed into the exchange by operators connecting instantly to the Betfair site.

The introduction of 'telbet' reinforced the advantage of exchanges versus the main market, raising the volume of business going through the exchange and making it possible for a Betfair customer to use his account when at the races or otherwise away from a computer. By pioneering telbet, Betfair extended its lead over other exchanges. By further boosting revenues, the move improved profits, return on capital and the ability to invest further in marketing, site improvement and attractive new betting products.

Betfair continued its intelligent innovation, with its distinctive 'exchange poker' game, in which the object is to guess which of five players is going to win a game. In 2006 came the 'Betfair casino', a host of innovative new games. It included the 'zero lounge', a series of games removing the house's edge, including a new type of roulette with no zero on the wheel. By inventing new, better-value games, Betfair again illustrates the golden rules.

★ The new games make the betting-exchange category even more attractive, reinforcing the reality of vastly superior value to the 'old' bookmaking industry, including its forays into online gaming.

★ They force competitors into an impossible catch-up game. All the best innovation space is constantly scooped by Betfair. If rivals copy, they simply pay visible homage to Betfair.

★ Providing better value in the new area of casino games

makes great business sense for Betfair, since the cost of developing the games is quickly amortised and they provide huge incremental volume and profit for Betfair, even while providing customers with vastly superior value. Profitable variation indeed.

Charles Schwab is another great illustration of star innovation. The firm was the first discount broker, providing a telephone service at a fraction of the price charged by traditional stockbrokers. The business remained a star through intelligent innovation.

★ *The first* discount broker to introduce instant confirmation of trades made by the customer. This removed the greatest obstacle to the new category of discount broking: was it really secure? could it really be trusted? Charles Schwab realised that it was not price alone that motivated its target customers, but rather *value*. Instant confirmation made discount broking attractive, providing a service that was reliable and eased customers' minds, at little cost to the firm.

★ *The first* discount broker to move large numbers of its customers to online trades, again providing the security of instant confirmation.

★ *The first* discount broker to provide 24/7 service.

★ *The first* discount broker to provide a cash-management account, making transfer of funds from (and to) customers' banks unnecessary. The Schwab One cash-management account, which comes with a Visa card and cheque privileges, is convenient for customers. It gets round the delay and hassle of moving money from traditional banks (with their slow response times and restricted hours of opening).

★ *The first* discount broker to help customers track their investments. Schwab's OneSource provides a monthly statement of all trades and investments made through the broker.

How do these illustrate the golden rules?

★ They proved that discount broking could mean *high service* as well as *cheap*.

★ They forced discount brokerage rivals into catch-up mode, reinforcing the respectability and comfort in the Charles Schwab brand, and making customers more reluctant to switch to another discount broker.

★ The innovations enabled Charles Schwab to avoid competing purely on price, and in many cases simultaneously to improve service *and* to make extra profits – profitable variation.

Has your venture mastered the innovation formula yet? Is the take-off truly secure? Will your venture fly higher and higher, or be shot down by a more innovative rival?

Conclusion: The way to take off

The take-off is a white-knuckle ride. If you manage it, the sky's the limit. If you hover above the ground and then fall back, you crash. The way to maximise your chance of take-off is to form four small teams – each comprising a founder and two other employees – charged with master-minding each element of take-off: customer attraction; the commercial formula for fat margins; delivery; and innovation. Start a weekly meeting for everyone on Monday morning or Friday afternoon, where each team gives a five-minute report and everyone else has five minutes for comments and questions. Progress and activities can be compared to the entrepreneurial guidelines distilled in this chapter. If the teams follow the guidelines, take-off will be more likely, smoother, faster and more enduring. Once you have taken off, the most wonderful vista – the world itself – is at your feet.

14

Evolve into a star

What I do, I understand.
Confucius

Is this your predicament? You're running a baby business. In reading this book, you realise with a growing sense of discomfort that your venture is not a star. You didn't invent a new niche and you are a follower. Or else you did invent a new category but it's not growing fast.

The chances are that your business is not a star. Fewer than 1 in 20 businesses are. You realise you'd be much better off with one of the very few that are stars. What do you do?

Is there a way of changing tack so that you evolve into a star? Should you persevere and hope that your existing business will prove at least moderately successful? Or give up, take what cash is left, and start anew?

By the end of this chapter, your mind will be made up.

Don't panic!

Recall that only two of my stars were born that way. The other three 'achieved stardom' or 'had stardom thrust upon them'.

If you set out to turn your venture into a star, and focus on this as the overriding imperative – the only thing that really matters – you have a head start on nearly everybody else: the people who don't know what a star is or who aren't seriously trying to make their venture a star. If you resolve to make your venture a star, you suddenly take a huge leap in your prospects, simply by making that decision. If you follow the guidelines in this chapter, and pursue stardom with iron ambition, you'll have a decent shot at making it.

If you evolve into a star, you'll be in good company. Not just because of my three stars. Many of the greatest stars we celebrate today had inauspicious beginnings.

How some famous stars evolved

Coca-Cola. This inspired name emerged from a brainstorming session held by John Pemberton and his three partners in 1886. Coca-Cola was highly descriptive – the main ingredients were coca leaf (containing cocaine) and kola nuts. Yet Coca-Cola was descended from a whole raft of drinks that Pemberton had created since the late 1860s. For nearly 20 years he concocted drink after drink – Globe Flower Cough Syrup, Extract of Stillingia, many other exotic brews. In 1885 he launched his first star, Pemberton's French Wine Coca. Laced with cocaine, the wine sold 888 bottles the first Saturday it appeared. It was only the prohibition of alcohol in Atlanta and Fulton County, effective from 1886, that led Pemberton to invent Coca-Cola as a 'dry' version.

IBM's roots go back to the Tabulating Machine Company incorporated in 1896 as a supplier of punch cards and machines for statistical analysis. IBM was late into the computer market. The first computer, ENIAC – Electronic Numerical Integrator and Computer – was unveiled at the University of Pennsylvania in 1946. UNIVAC emerged as the commercial arm of the project and in 1950 Remington Rand acquired UNIVAC, becoming the undisputed leader in computers. IBM wrested star status from UNIVAC through a tortuous evolution, after it won a contract to develop computers for the US Air Force.

WPP Group, now one of the world's leading communications companies, began life as Wire and Plastic Products Plc, making shopping carts for supermarkets. WPP now owns star businesses in several advertising, PR and marketing-research segments.

Few firms have tested the limits of evolution as thoroughly as *Nokia Corporation*. Started as a Finnish pulp mill in 1865, the Nokia brand was then applied to a range of rubber products, notably wellington boots and other footwear. Nokia tried its hand at paper products, bicycle and car tyres, electrical cables, electricity, TVs and PCs. None of these were stars. In the 1970s, Nokia began to develop mobile (or cell) phones and emerged as the leader in this fast-growth market in the 1980s. Nokia then quit all other activities to focus entirely on cell phones. Today Nokia has its 80/80 rule – 80 per cent market share worth $80 billion. When you are frustrated with your umpteenth attempt to evolve into a star venture, remember Nokia.

William Wrigley started a soap factory. As a promotion, he gave away baking powder. Customers loved the baking powder, so *Wrigley's* evolved into a firm making baking powder. Then they gave away chewing gum with the baking powder, and the gum proved more popular. Before long the firm made only gum. Wrigley's had been a follower in soap and baking powder, but became the global winner in gum.

Finally, *Starbucks*. Recall that Starbucks began in 1971 selling coffee beans and equipment. It didn't sell drinks until the late 1980s, and wasn't a star until more than 20 years after it started.

Could you evolve into a star?

Are you Number Two in a high-growth market – BCG's 'question mark' position?

The issue here is simple. Can you overtake the leader? Your chances are greater if:

★ your market share is not far below the leader's;

★ you are gaining on the leader;

★ the leader makes an unexpected blunder;

★ the niche is young;

★ market positions are volatile and one or two large customers can swing it;

★ the market is growing very fast;

★ you understand the customers in the niche better;

★ even though you are in the same market, your approach is *different* and customers like it better;

★ your people have better empathy with the customers;

★ your approach has *fatter margins* than the leader, or would do so if you had the same volume of business;

★ you are better financed than the leader;

★ objective observers say your product is better;

★ the leader's advantage rests on distribution advantages that you can gradually overcome;

★ key employees from the leader are defecting to you;

★ the leader is only dimly aware of the threat you pose.

Beware of over-optimism. Most Number Twos imagine that they can overhaul the Number One. Most Number Twos don't. The Number One is there for a reason. Having got there, they are in pole position. Inertia, better-known or better-loved brands, customer relationships, market knowledge and usually higher margins sustain the leader and give it unfair advantages. Blind tests over the past 30 years have consistently given Pepsi-Cola the edge over Coca-Cola. Yet in the US and most other markets Coke continues to outsell Pepsi by more than two to one.

By and large, in settled markets, Number Two can't win against Number One. The Number Two wins only when the leader makes a silly mistake (like Filofax pricing to the skies). As Number Two, you can be as clever and creative as you like, but your fate is not in your own hands. For you to win, the leader must blunder. You can't count on that.

The best test is practical. If your market share is not increasing quite fast, and that of the Number One is not falling, then you are unlikely to close the gap.

If you carry on doing the same things, you won't win. Even doing the same things much better – better than in the past, better than the opposition – you *still* won't win.

Do something different. Try a number of approaches. If doing something different within your current niche doesn't work, then do something different outside it. Try to evolve into a star.

Are you the niche leader, but the market isn't growing fast?

If your venture is young and you're the leader, you probably invented the niche. The issue isn't so much the opposition, but whether the niche itself will take off.

You face Catch-22. You can't become profitable unless you grow fast. But you can't rely on market momentum to help you grow. The market won't acquire momentum unless you do something different – something dramatic to get noticed – but you don't have the cash to do this. You're stuck in a backwater and the clock is ticking. If you carry on like this you'll run out of cash. If you spend more cash, the hour of reckoning will probably close in on you.

Your basic problem is market apathy. Nobody cares whether you live or die.

The niche is not viable. You thought you had a star business, but you don't. Probably you don't have a business at all. (The only exception is when the venture makes a profit and is cash-positive already. In this case, you have a small business that will remain small. Are you happy with that?)

Your position is desperate. If you have unspent cash, consider giving up and returning the cash – especially if a large chunk of it is yours!

The only sensible alternative is to evolve into a star.

What do you have to lose?
You might just win, and win big. Even if you don't become a star, the attempt may help. You'll probably get closer to useful customers, and develop unique and valuable venture DNA.

Four linked steps to evolve into a star

1. GO BACK TO THE DRAWING BOARD
Return to the chapters (9 and 10) on creating your star. This may feel like sliding down a snake but in fact you'll have a head start over a new team coming fresh to the star-design exercise. At least you have some experience, some capabilities, exposure to customers and the market generally. As the saga of LEK shows, even wrong-headed strategy and positioning – even the loss of your main customers – can be turned to your advantage. You are already a player, already in the thick of events as they swirl around you. If

you spot some of what is happening ahead of rivals, and adapt your capabilities to poorly served customer groups, adversity can be your trump card.

2. MIGRATE YOUR PRODUCT

LEK had to move away from 'standard' strategy towards analysis of competitors. This led to 'relative cost position' and 'acquisition analysis'.

Your task is to find a unique product or service, one not offered *in that form* by anyone else. Your raw material is, of course, what you and the rest of your industry do already. Tweak it in ways that could generate an attractive new product. The ideal product is:

★ close to something you already do very well, or could do very well;

★ something customers are already groping towards or you know they will like;

★ capable of being 'automated' or otherwise done at low cost, by using a new process (cutting out costly steps, such as self-service), a new channel (the phone or Internet), new lower-cost employees (LEK's 'kids', highly educated people in India), new raw materials (cheap resins, free data from the Internet), excess capacity from a related industry (especially manufacturing capacity), new technology or simply new ideas;

★ able to be 'orchestrated' by your firm while you yourself are doing as little as possible;

★ really valuable or appealing to a clearly defined customer group – therefore commanding fatter margins;

★ difficult for any rival to provide as well or as cheaply – ideally something they cannot or would not want to do.

Because you are already in business, you can experiment with new products in a way that someone thinking of starting a venture cannot do. Sometimes the answer is breathtakingly simple. The Filofax system didn't start to take off until David Collischon provided 'filled organisers' – a wallet with a standard set of papers installed. What could you do that is simple, costs you little or nothing and yet is hugely attractive to customers?

Ask customers if they would like something different. Mock up a prototype; show it around. Brainstorm new ideas. Evolution needs false starts. If an idea isn't working, don't push it uphill. If a possible new product resonates at all, keep tweaking it until you have a winner.

At the same time . . .

3. MIGRATE YOUR DNA

New products require new capabilities. Equally, new products can *result* from the unique character and living expansion of your firm. No two species are identical. Neither are two ventures. The mix of founders and early employees is unique. Nobody will ever do things quite the way you do. *The more different you can make your firm, the better.* Intelligently, of course,

★ hire and promote people who have similar attitudes to the target market;

★ hire people who get on well with each other and go the extra mile for customers and colleagues;

★ hire people who have a high ratio of smarts to cost – younger or from neglected talent pools;

★ hire risk-takers, experimenters, explorers, oddballs, and those with a restless spirit;

★ train on the job; team novices with senior role models; concentrate on the few things customers like most, that can be done with least effort and cost;

★ make your venture bright, quirky, colourful, distinctive, fun and highly commercial – thrilling customers *at a high profit* for the firm.

Encourage smart experiments at every level, in every way, at every time. Make it a way of life in your firm. Then, sooner or later, your star *will* emerge.

LEK did not start by migrating its product. First we migrated its DNA, then we created products we were uniquely able to sell. This goes against the grain, but it works!

At the same time . . .

4. MIGRATE YOUR TARGET CUSTOMER BASE

Every star venture wants to end up with a unique set of

customers, ideally suited to its products and DNA. To migrate towards your ideal target customers, identify:

★ suitable customers you know already or could easily access;

★ customers who are disgruntled with their existing suppliers;

★ customers who need a product you can envision, not currently being provided;

★ customers who give you pleasure;

★ customers who aren't price-sensitive;

★ customers you know you can help most;

★ fast-growth companies;

★ big and profitable companies;

★ loyal customers, who hate to switch suppliers;

★ customers with whom you can build a 'thick' relationship;

★ customers who'll recommend you to big customers;

★ people within organisations at the most senior level you can possibly reach.

Linked migration

Your product, your DNA, your target customers – these comprise the 'migration trinity'. As you move away from your existing product, DNA and customers, grasp the opportunity to do two great things together:

★ move away from your competitors' products, DNA, and customer groups; *and*

★ move your new products, DNA and customers ever closer together.

Figure 14.1 shows the position before migration – your products, DNA, and customers are similar to those of your main competitors.

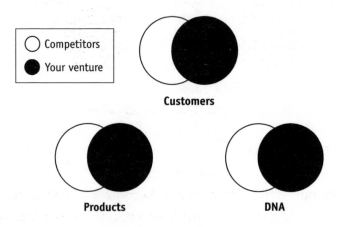

Figure 14.1 Before migration

Figure 14.2 shows the effect of migration. Your venture's products, DNA and customer groups move:

★ away from those you started with;

★ away from their proximity to competitors' products, DNA and customer groups; and

★ close together.

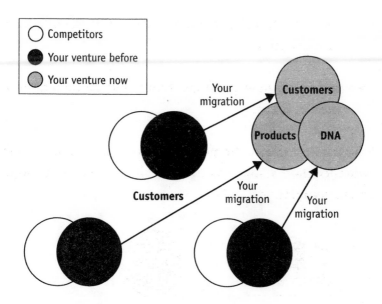

Figure 14.2 After migration

Conclusion

For non-star ventures, try to become a star. Venturers of the world, rise up – you have nothing to lose but your chains, and a wonderful world to win.

How? By boldly going where no firm has gone before. Invent unknown products. Discover uncharted customer groups. Create a new type of firm.

This is evolution. This is the root of all progress. From the simple process of divergence, new ventures, new products and new wealth are endlessly spawned. Creating a new species of firm is the highest and most rewarding art of the entrepreneur.

15

The importance of unreasonable expectations

High expectations are the key to everything.
Sam Walton

Reasonable expectations are fine for reasonably attractive ventures – say, your typical cash cow. But star businesses are unusually attractive. They require unreasonable expectations. Otherwise you leave enormous piles of cash on the table.

Stars constitute under 5 per cent of all businesses, ever. But stars contribute over 95 per cent of long-term value, and probably at least 120 per cent of the cash ever generated. You wouldn't treat a budding concert pianist the same as the chap who plonks away in a bar, nor a potential Wimbledon champion like the average youngster at your local tennis club. Nor should star businesses be treated like normal ones. Stars are abnormal and should be treated abnormally.

What determines the long-term value of a star business? Very largely, the growth. OK, the profit margin matters, but even doubling the margin has far less influence on what the business is eventually worth than the growth rate and hence the ultimate level of sales.

At least 90 per cent or more of a star's value over the long haul derives from its growth. For businesses that grow for a very long time, such as McDonald's and Coca-Cola, the number is over 99 per cent.

Nearly everyone hugely underestimates the growth potential of stars. Typically, the growth potential is under-rated not by 100 or 200 per cent but by 1,000 per cent or 10,000 per cent. If you don't believe this, think about McDonald's. Mac and Dick McDonald sold out in 1961 for $2.7 million. Today the firm is worth $48 billion, which is 1,777,000 times higher. They received 0.001 per cent of its value today, missing out on 99.9 per cent. To be sure, we need to adjust for 46 years of inflation and a return on top. What stands out, though, is that the brothers had no idea how far their firm could go.

They are not alone. Almost all founders of star businesses underestimate their growth potential and value. Two action implications: never sell a star business (while it remains a star); and demand much faster growth.

What growth rate should you target?

How fast did my stars grow?

Belgo grew its sales by 20–30 per cent a year in the first decade. Plymouth Gin grew between 20 and 40 per cent annually when I was involved. Filofax grew by a shade over 20 per cent a year from 1990 to 1997, on top of annual growth of 111 per cent from 1982 to 1987. LEK grew at 100 per cent a year in my time. Betfair grew at 100–300 per cent in its first three years, before slowing to a more normal 30–50 per cent annual rate.

Icons of American business such as Ford, GE, McDonald's, IBM, Xerox, Disney, Mars and Intel all grew at between 20 and 50 per cent a year for decades. Coca-Cola grew at more than 10 per cent a year for a century. More recently, stars such as Microsoft, Starbucks, Amazon and Google have grown at 20–50 per cent a year.

Aim to grow your star at least 20–30 per cent a year. During the first decade, 50–100 per cent is more like it. Another way: take your current growth rate, and aim to double it.

SEVEN WAYS TO MAKE YOUR STAR GROW FASTER
Let us starting with the most important.

1. Raise the target growth rate
Whatever growth target you have, it's almost certainly too low. Stars have a commanding position in a high-growth market. They are in the best position to grow fast and to accelerate the market growth. Stars should never grow less fast than their category.

2. Expand geographically
This was *the* secret of British business in the nineteenth century and of American, Japanese and Korean firms in the last century. Most star ventures should aim to conquer the world.

3. Innovate – new value
Stars typically blast off by providing a neglected group of

customers with a new deal that they love – a different mix of product attributes that add up to great value. Yet too many star ventures don't recreate new value year after year. Part of Betfair's extraordinary growth can be explained by features such as in-running betting, which had never been tried before. Growth comes from deepening the relationship with customers, offering them more and more.

4. Innovate – new products

The rule of thumb for new products is 'few, big, core'. A multitude of minor products typically diffuses effort and profitability. One or two blockbusters that can be sold to the same core customer base are much better. In the twentieth century, Coca-Cola derived enormous growth from just two new products – Fanta (which, curiously, was invented in Nazi Germany) and TaB/Diet Coke.

5. Innovate – new channels

As with Betfair's use of the phone as well as the Internet, the same product can often be sold in much larger volume by using new distribution channels.

6. Innovate – new customers

This is riskier, because it steps outside the precious core market that you have created. New customers may want adaptations to your product that don't play to your strengths. The safest way to interest new customers is to take the existing product and sell it to a new group of customers who are *most like your existing customers*. A classic gambit is gradually to move upmarket or downmarket. Honda motorcycles, for example, established themselves with buyers of scooters and small bikes before gradually tackling the traditional market for larger machines.

7. Incremental acquisitions

Acquisitions are the riskiest route. They take attention away from the core market and diverge from the unique mix of DNA, products and customers that have made the star venture so successful. Acquisitions can be useful if they are small and very close to the existing core market. At Filofax, after we sorted out the core business in the early 1990s, we moved on to make a number of acquisitions. Those that were closest to the core business – such as the acquisition of Filofax's distributors in several countries – were successful. Those that were less related – including a greetings-card firm – were not. We would have done much better to forget acquisitions and focus on innovation in the base business.

FOUR WAYS *NOT* TO GROW YOUR STAR VENTURE

1. **Diversification** – don't stray beyond your heartland!

2. **Unrelated acquisitions** – never!

3. **Moving outside your core function or customer group** – Filofax's focus on fashion led to neglect of the core customers who simply wanted to be better organised.

4. **Introducing unrelated products** – as when Coca-Cola moved unprofitably into orange juice and health drinks.

Invest, invest, invest?

The classic prescription for star businesses is to 'invest, invest, invest' so that they grow as fast as possible. Is this still relevant today? Does it fit with my experience of making money? And what type of 'investment'?

One way that old-time investment is less necessary is in factories, production and operations generally. The original 1960s BCG perspective was framed by a rather traditional view of big business (already losing its relevance then), where investment in hard physical assets was essential. This is a long story and we shouldn't get distracted by it[16] – the nub here is that you should generally 'outsource' as much of your operations as possible, retaining only the few things that you do uniquely well. In particular, get other people to make things for you.

Since you probably won't be investing in factories, offices or other physical cash sinks, what's left is *expense investment* – the costs of your people, plus external marketing. The joy of stars is that they take modest investment to get to cash break even. Thereafter, investment can be funded out of the star's own cash flow.

Betfair is worth at least £1.54 billion today, but it took only about £2.5 million (most of which I provided) to get it to cash break even, and all the funds for expansion since have been internally generated.[17] To invest £2.5 million to

---

[16] Anyone interested in the transformation of our economy over the past 50 years can read my interpretation in Richard Koch and Chris Smith (2006), *Suicide of the West* (London: Continuum), Chapter 5.

[17] It is true that 3 per cent of new shares were issued to Softbank in April 2006, but this was simply because not enough shares were available from Betfair shareholders to satisfy the stake Softbank wanted. At the time, Betfair had a large cash pile (as it still does) and did not need the money.

get a return of £1.54 billion implies a return on cash of more than 600 times!

Be willing to accept lower profits to build a dominant market position As long as you remain cash–positive, short-term profits are totally irrelevant to the long-term value of the business. Build by far the best product and service in your niche, moving further away ahead of would-be rivals.

The star invests in its own growth; the plaudits of customers are expressed in growth. Growth is the means of success and the evidence of success. The things that make a star successful and valuable are difference, innovation and growth; but the greatest of these is growth.

Star ventures deserve star people

It's not wasteful to have ordinary people work in ordinary businesses. But star ventures deserve the very best people in all functions – marketing, technology, research, new product development, selling, operations, finance and innovation of all kinds. True, star businesses can get by with average or even below-average executives, because the strength of the concept is so great. Yet the difference between a star venture with ordinary people and one with extraordinary people is amazing. Ventures such as eBay and Google are fantastic star concepts executed extremely well. The additional cost of extraordinary people is dust in the scales compared with the benefit for star businesses.

But here is the rub. Finding excellent people for your star venture is tricky. Your money is not enough. You need to be subtler and go for people of a particular *stamp*.

★ Hire people who have worked in very fast-growth firms, preferably in a star venture. They alone understand what it takes to grow fast. They alone will have demanding enough standards of growth for themselves and the rest of you.

★ Hire people who match the venture's DNA and will fit in. I could tell you of terrible mistakes I've made in hiring apparently great people who didn't understand growth and didn't respect the culture of the firms they joined and had to be fired at great expense and inconvenience – but I am afraid of libel lawyers, so if you want to learn more you'll have to buy me a drink. Suffice it to say I have learned my lesson. Trust me – don't hire anyone not fully *simpatico*.

★ Control the recruitment process yourself and involve a large number of colleagues in each decision. Don't trust headhunters, whose main concern is to shift their inventory. Potential new hires should see a cross section of the organisation, including quite junior people. Don't allow any early interviewers to give an opinion before everyone has interviewed the candidate – otherwise herd mentality may take over. Do not employ anyone who gets blackballed by, say, two out of ten employees, even if the dissenters are the most junior.

★ Hire to raise the average. Ideally, each new recruit should be in the top 10 per cent of existing employees.

That way the firm will constantly get better and better.

Put immense time and effort into recruitment. You will avoid costly blunders (such as I have often made) and reap where you sow.

The value of conflict

A healthy tension and conflict between the star venture executives and the owners is a good thing, and in my experience necessary to maximise the value of the star. Unreasonable expectations are not likely to emerge, without some prodding and pushing, from the executives themselves. Even when they are large shareholders, exec-utives are intrinsically biased towards the management team rather than the owners of the business (including themselves). I am not a psychologist, so can't explain this trait, but I am positive it exists and is one of the main menaces to realising the value of any star venture. Executives may want to expand the business fast but they would be superhuman if they set themselves the most demanding targets conceivable. Yet, I argue, only the most extraordinary targets can realise the potential value of a star business. If you look at firms such as Coca-Cola, McDonald's, IBM and Microsoft, you see how nearly everyone grossly underestimated their long-term growth potential.

The trouble with founders who remain executives is that it is very difficult to shift them, even when they are palpably acting in the interests of the managers rather than the owners. Not all founders are like this – Bill Gates and Jeff Bezos are heroic exceptions – but most of the ones I've met are. In fact, it may be a condition of a star venture's reaching its potential that the founders consistently take the side of the owners and drive for maximum growth, or else they step aside gracefully. If you work in a star venture, what about your founders?

There is a fatal flaw in corporate governance, in that the owners of a business are not normally strongly represented on the outside board. In the UK, a listed company is actually discouraged from having board members who are significant shareholders, because they are classed as being 'not independent'. This is lunacy (and a good reason for star ventures to steer clear of the stock market, for as long as possible and preferably for ever). To paraphrase Adam Smith, you can't expect people who aren't owners – either as executives or non-executive board members – to have the interests of the owners fully at heart. It is not just the owners who suffer as a result. So do all employees, because any firm not harried and pressed by extremely demanding owners will never reach its full potential, likely nowhere near it. The difference – and forgive me for repeating – is not marginal. The gap between a star venture's reaching its potential and its 'doing well enough' is a difference of hundreds, thousands or millions of percentage points.

The value of collaboration: changing the role of founders

If there is value in conflict between owners and founders, there is also value in collaboration, especially when it comes to changing the role of founders. If you are a substantial owner, what do you do if the founder or founders are proving unable to achieve the growth that you want? One way is to try to persuade them to step aside. If they won't budge, then what? You have a choice. You either pursue the point remorselessly, forcing other directors to decide whether the founder should be fired, or you try a more subtle strategy, of changing the founder's role gradually, slice by slice. Often, there is no need to remove the founder, if somebody else is given a clear mandate to accelerate the growth.

Belgo provides an excellent illustration of this point, because I failed to grasp it at the time. After three years of stunning success, I was disappointed that we were not opening new outlets more quickly. The pattern became clear. The guys would find a new site, we'd all look at it, we'd run the numbers, and then decide to go ahead. Then ... nothing much would happen. There were always problems with the site or the plans. Eventually, André and Denis would say that the site wouldn't work and we'd go back to square one.

Eventually I became so frustrated that we decided to sell the business – rather earlier than I would have liked – because we could not agree on the growth expectations (mine remaining firmly unreasonable). Somebody else could expand the chain faster than we could. This worked very well for us all financially, but I still regret the lost opportunity to expand the Belgo star ourselves.

Later I reflected on what had happened. The truth is that finding, designing and opening new restaurants is a hell of a job. Though they were happy to continue with what they were really great at – imbuing each new outlet with excitement and the authentic Belgo feel, nurturing the staff, building a corps of loyal customers for each location and getting publicity for the group through amusing antics – they were tired of the hard slog that preceded each opening. Why didn't they say so? Why was I too stupid to realise? Why didn't we face the truth and delegate finding and preparing new Belgos to somebody else, brought in for that role? The founders would have enjoyed a congenial life and worked their magic to ever greater degrees. They would have stayed for the long term. And I could have had the growth I wanted.

Conclusion

Growth is everything. Star ventures should grow at least 20–50 per cent each year in their first decade. This rate of advance is so far beyond most people's experience that enormous effort is required to impose 'unreasonable expectations'. All progress, said George Bernard Shaw, comes from unreasonable people. This truth should be engraved on the hearts of everyone who works in or owns a star venture.

16

The fading star

You don't know what you've got 'til it's gone.
Joni Mitchell

What if your star begins to fade? According to the star-business theory, this is a grave state of affairs. While a star, the venture is enormously valuable. If it ceases to be a star, its value may plunge.

How can this be? It seems a rather draconian theory. It rather goes against common sense that a movement in the market growth rate – say from 25 per cent a year down to 5 per cent – should mean the value of the star crumbles. It also appears extreme to say that loss of market leadership, even when not accompanied by a loss of sales, is nothing less than a disaster.

Yet it is so. That loss of star status is a business tragedy can be substantiated, both in theory and in practice.

The theory

A star venture is immensely valuable because it has four attributes together.

1. It operates in a high-growth market, and so, over a long period of time, and so long as it holds its market share, will grow its sales immensely.

2. It is the market leader, and so will be highly profitable, either because it has lower costs than rivals (able to spread fixed costs over greater volume), or because as the popular choice it commands higher prices, or for both reasons.

3. With greater experience than rivals, and with costs as a percentage of sales tending to decline, both its percentage profits (over sales) and profits relative to rivals will tend to increase. Profits also rise because of the market growth, but profits should rise faster than sales. In a normal market, profitability is constrained by competition. In a star market, profitability is constrained only by what customers will pay.

4. Because of high and rising profitability, and because rivals can't force you to make cash-guzzling investments, stars are likely to throw off lots of cash. Unusually for a growing venture, growth can normally be financed out of cash flow. The owners' equity is not diluted by the need to raise money and issue new shares. All growth goes to existing shareholders and none to new ones.

It's hard to grasp intuitively how wonderful this combination of benefits is. Let's run some numbers.

Company A is a star and maintains its lead in a market growing at 25 per cent. It starts with sales of $10 million and a return on sales of 20 per cent, netting $2 million pretax. After 30 per cent tax, it has profits of $1.4 million. Because its profits are growing fast the value of the company is estimated to be 25 times its after-tax earnings (in financial-speak, it is on a price-to-earnings ratio, or PE, of 25). This makes Company A worth $35 million.

Company B (in a different market) starts off in the same position as Company A, also worth $35 million. But Company B is a fading star. Its market growth rate falls to 5 per cent a year. The firm does not lose market share but it ends up as a *cash cow*.

After 10 years, the magic of compound arithmetic has taken Company A to sales of $93 million. Because of greater experience and cost sharing and lack of effective competition, by Year 10 the firm's return on sales has risen to 40 per cent. Its profits are $37.3 million before tax and $26.1 million after. Taking the same PE of 25, the venture is now worth $652 million, nearly 19 times more than before.

For Company B, the cash cow, sales have risen to only $16.3 million. Its return on sales remains 20 per cent and its profits are $3.3 million before tax, $2.3 million after. Because of the lower growth in earnings, its PE has fallen to 12.5, half the previous level. Company B is now valued at $28.5 million, less than 10 years earlier, when its star promise gave it a higher valuation. Company B is worth less than a twentieth of company A, all because market growth is down.

Company C (also in a different market from Companies A and B) starts in the same position as the two other firms. Company C suffers competition and loses its star position.

At the start, C has 40 per cent of the market and its nearest rival has 20 per cent. By Year 10, these positions have flip-flopped and Company C is now a *question-mark* business. The market continues to grow at 25 per cent a year – all that's changed is the loss of market share. But that has some bad consequences. The return on sales falls to 10 per cent and the PE ratio to 12.5 times earnings. Also hurting the owners of Company C is the shift from being cash-positive to cash-negative, so the venture needs further cash to support its growth. The firm has to raise money from shareholders; the original shareholders, if they put no more money in, have their shareholding cut in half.

When the arithmetic is worked through for Year 10, Company C has sales of $46.6 million and pretax profits of $4.7 million, which is $3.3 million after tax. Multiply $3.3 million by 12.5 and the firm is worth $41.3 million. But only half of this goes to the original shareholders, so their stake is worth $20.6 million, much less than ten years earlier and less than one-thirtieth of the value of star Company A.

To recap the position for the original shareholders:

Company	Initial value	10-year value	Started as	Ended as
A	$35m	$652m	Star	Star
B	$35m	$28.5	Star	Cash cow
C	$35m	$20.6m	Star	Question mark

The Year 10 value for the shareholders compared with the start is:

Company		
A	Star	1,863% of starting position
B	Cash cow	81% of starting position
C	Question mark	59% of starting position

The Year 10 value for shareholders compared with the value of Company A is:

Company		
A	Star	100%
B	Cash cow	4%
C	Question mark	3%

This is without contemplating the worst and ultimately most likely outcome for the fallen star – that it becomes a nearly worthless dog.

The practice

Nearly every firm that multiplies its value does so because it is a star business.

We've seen dozens of examples of such dramatic increases for star ventures. Can you name a single case of a venture in normal competitive markets – excluding natural resources such as oil and land – that has increased in value much faster than other companies and is not a star business?

On the other hand, there have been many instances

where very valuable star businesses have suffered after losing their star position. Ford Motor Corporation was one of the most valuable firms in the world around 1920 before losing its star position. It's now a financially weak dog.

High-technology British firms such as ICL in computers, Thorn-EMI in medical electronics and Psion in electronic organisers were once highly valued stars, only to lose their leadership positions and most of their value. Almost the whole of the British motorcycle industry collapsed after losing its star position to American and Japanese firms. Firestone's value imploded in the 1970s after it lost its star position in making car tyres.

Far worse tragedy befell Xerox Corporation. Xerox was one of the most valuable corporations in the world in the 1960s and 1970s, based on its dominance of the high-growth office-copier market. Xerox invented the plain-paper photocopier in 1959, and by 1965 its revenues had grown to more than $500 million, equivalent to $3 billion today. But Xerox was a star that faded badly. By 1982, Xerox had lost its lead in the mid-range copier market to Canon. Between 1976 and 1982, Canon introduced more than 90 new copier models. Canon then grabbed Xerox's star position in high-end colour copiers.

It gets worse. In 1970, Xerox PARC research centre was opened in Palo Alto, California. It rapidly developed a vast treasure trove of new technology that could have made Xerox the most valuable company in history. Within three years, the PARC boffins had created the Xerox Alto, a small minicomputer equivalent to a workstation and personal computer. Xerox's top brass thought it had no sales potential. Xerox PARC went on to invent Windowstype software, the mouse, the laser printer, the paperless office and Ethernet. These were all potential star ventures that were never commercialised by Xerox.

In 1979 Steve Jobs, the Apple Computer boss, visited Xerox PARC. Jobs immediately saw the potential for the PC and the mouse. For many years now Xerox has been a low-growth corporation and its market value is currently only $14 billion, a small fraction of the value of the many star companies exploiting its inventions. Apple alone is worth $65 billion, nearly five times as much as Xerox.

When Filofax faded – twice!

Filofax lost its star status twice – in the later 1980s and again ten years later. We've seen how a cut-price rival threatened its market leadership, and how we beat off that threat. Within four years, its shares were trading at an all-time high of 279p, some 21 times the low point of 13p in 1990.

By the later 1990s, however, the market growth rate for paper organisers fell from 10–20 per cent down to around 5 per cent a year. Filofax became a cash cow, still profitable, but not as valuable. When we sold the business in 1998 for 210p per share, that was well off the peak and we were lucky to get that much.

As long as market leadership is retained, the transition from a star business to a cash cow, as the market slows down, is not nearly as bad as the transition from star to question mark by losing market leadership. Yet market deceleration is more difficult to deal with. Provided the threat from a competitor is realised in time, provided the leader is willing to change its way of doing business to outflank the upstart – for sure, two big ifs – then stars can usually stay stars. Loss of market growth is more difficult to reverse.

Could Filofax have revived market growth? There were some countries, notably Sweden and Switzerland, where organisers in general and Filofax in particular had huge prominence and promotion. Some board members argued that, if Filofax put the same effort into other major markets, we could accelerate the market again. Others noted that, although Sweden and Switzerland had much higher per capita penetration of organisers, they still reached maturity at the same time as other countries.

I usually favour action to revive flagging markets, because a star is so much more valuable than a cash cow. In this case, though, it was probably mission impossible. In the late 1990s, more and more Filofax customers used their mobile phones (and to a lesser extent electronic organisers) to store phone numbers and addresses. From there it was a short hop to using electronic diaries as well.

Never sell a star, or a fading star that can recover leadership. But an ex-star should be sold before the damage is fully evident.

Betfair in peril

Now that Betfair is extremely valuable it is hard to realise how much jeopardy it faced in the early days. The traditional big bookmakers in England lobbied hard and long to get betting exchanges outlawed. When they lost this battle they switched to lobbying for additional taxes on both the exchanges and their users. All these attempts eventually failed. But the most serious threat Betfair faced in its very early days, shortly after I invested, was from Flutter, a rival exchange.

I made my investment in April 2001, when Betfair outgunned Flutter 10 to 1. Flutter had $45 million of venture capital to play with. Betfair had been started on a shoestring and had almost no cash left before I invested my relatively paltry £1.5 million. Most observers rated Flutter's technology superior to Betfair's. Flutter's chief technology officer, an astute American called David Yu, was masterminding a steady assault on Betfair's market share. I suspected that Betfair was losing market share to Flutter, but this was denied by Betfair management. It later became clear that the loss of market share was even more serious than I had suspected. From being roughly ten times bigger than Flutter at the start of 2001, Betfair was only three times bigger by the end of the year. With this trend, Flutter would soon have overtaken Betfair.

How could Betfair not have noticed what was happening? Well, remember that Betfair was growing at more than 30 per cent a month. It was doubling in size every quarter. How much faster should a firm want to grow? How much faster *could* it grow? Besides, most market leaders believe they are much better than their competitors, so it is hard to believe that they are closing the gap. As is usually the case in new market niches, there was no market-share information available. How could Betfair not have noticed? Very easily.

I felt that we absolutely had to keep our star position. But how? To beat Flutter back would take a great deal of cash that we didn't have. Even if we could raise more money, the venture capitalists would take most of the company from us. The simpler and more elegant solution was to merge the two exchanges, which we did in December 2001.

Clearly, both firms stood to gain from this move, although, to be honest, Betfair benefited more than Flutter. Betfair shareholders took 70 per cent of the combined group, Flutter shareholders 30 per cent. David Yu became Betfair's head of technology, and eventually its chief executive. I breathed a great sigh of relief.

The merger was codenamed 'Snowball' because we hoped that combining liquidity would lead to a snowball effect. So it proved. Betfair's monthly growth rate jumped from around 30 per cent to 65 per cent. Much more important to me, however, was that Betfair went from a faltering star to a dominant star. From having a lead of three times its nearest rival it now had a lead of ten times, an edge maintained ever since.

What if your star begins to fade?

If the threat is from a rival, find a way to reverse that dynamic and go clear again. Do whatever it takes. Identify why the rival is gaining and then outflank it. Become paranoid about your competition. Think whether you could invent a new star position that is adjacent to your current venture. If there is only one serious challenger in your niche, consider a merger. In the long run, however, your salvation requires enormous, sustained innovation and being able to deliver superb value to your core customers.

If the problem is falling market growth, you have a choice. If the market slow-down is inevitable, accept it gracefully and perhaps sell your venture. If you think you can get market growth back above 10 per cent a year, do so.

Conclusion

Typically, the value of a star venture grows greatly. If it loses its star position, the lost opportunity is huge. Therefore, move heaven and earth to keep your star in the ascendant.

Summary

WHAT HAVE WE DISCOVERED?

Only puny secrets need protection. Big discoveries are protected by public incredulity.
Marshall McLuhan

What will make you successful?

★ Cast aside vanity. It is not your ability.

★ Cast aside puritanism. It is not how hard you work.

★ Cast aside your social aspirations. It is not the people you work with.

What will make you successful is being in the right place. Finding the right place to work or invest. Finding an unusual type of business, but one you can always find if you know exactly what to look for.

Finding a star venture. Maybe inventing one. Or simply being an early employee or investor in one.

There *is* a free lunch, if you know where to look. Through lucky experience, and trial and error, I've discovered how wonderful star businesses are, and how to find them.

So what exactly is a star business?

I was 25 when I stumbled across the 'star' concept. It had been invented by Bruce Henderson, founder of the Boston Consulting Group, a few years before I went to work there.

A star business, Bruce said, has two qualities:

★ it must be the leader in its market niche; and

★ the market niche must be growing fast.

In the early days, a business may be obscure and very small. But, if it satisfies these two conditions, you can be confident that it will one day be very big and valuable.

You can use the definition of a star business to create one quite deliberately.

The power of the star idea

Ever since I learned the secret of star ventures from Bruce Henderson, I've worked and invested in star ventures. I've had the time of my life. In the last three decades I've been involved with five star ventures. All have been notably successful. The average return has been ten times the money I put in. The best so far has been 53 times.

The star formula really works. This is not just my experience. It turns out that every very successful firm, almost without exception, is or was a star venture.

The trick is to spot the star venture when it is still under the radar, but already clearly a star – the leader in a high-growth niche. Go to work in the star, or put cash into it. Or invent your own star.

Once you realise the power of stars, your working life is transformed. Believe in the star idea. Act on it. It will set you free.

Stars are for everyone

Stars are not just for people who want to be entrepreneurs. Stars are for everyone who works. If you are not working in a star venture, look around and find one to work for. Ideally one that's just started, has just a handful of employees, but is expanding fast.

It's much more fun working for a star. You'll learn more. You'll develop new skills. You'll be Somebody. You'll get promoted more quickly. Before long, you'll be paid more and are likely to get fat bonuses. And share options. And the opportunity to buy shares as an employee could easily make you rich.

There is a myth about entrepreneurs, that they are lone rangers, visionaries, the authors of their own success. In some ways it's a useful myth because it gives romance to business. There is a lot more romance and fun in business than most people realise, so anything that gives it glamour is good.

Yet the myth of the entrepreneur suffers from one draw-back.

It's not true.

There is never just one key person in a venture that grows fast and big. Excepting small ventures that are a founder's personal vehicle and remain small, the character of the venture derives not from one or two people but from the interactions of the first employees, usually the first dozen or score of people. The firm's DNA derives from its early employees, their ideas and actions, not just those of the founder or founders.

All these early employees are really entrepreneurs. The lonely entrepreneur is a myth. The many-headed entre-preneur is the reality.

Even if you've never thought of becoming an entrepre-neur, even if you could never think of starting a business, you can still become an entrepreneur! By becoming one of the first employees, you share in making a venture take off. Believe me, nothing is so much fun, and nothing deepens you more. If you make megabucks, it's not just because you have lucked out. It is also because you have changed. The experience of working in a star venture will transform you.

The art of creating stars

Is saying you should search for a star venture just saying that you should start a very successful business?

Not at all. The star idea is unusual, specific, and stops you wasting time.

Most businesses do not lead their niche. Few niches manage to grow 10 per cent a year.

Between 95 and 99 per cent of new ventures are not stars. For every 20 ideas you have, you can confidently junk 19 of them, because they won't be ideas for a star venture. This saves an awful lot of money, sweat, toil and tears.

Star ventures are rare. The requirements are difficult. Why, then, do I say that creating a great new star business is possible?

Because you have a head start if you know precisely what you are looking for. I've codified what I know, the knowledge from looking for star ventures, from sometimes finding them and sometimes not. I think I now know how to go about it. And I've set it all down so you can create your own star.

Born stars versus 'stardom thrust upon them'

Two of my five ventures, Belgo and Betfair, were stars from the start. They created new niches that grew very fast. My other three stars achieved stardom after their initial years.

Filofax didn't become a star until the late 1970s, more than half a century after it started. David Collischon added a new dimension – that of fashion accessory – to the personal organiser. David showed how a cash cow can be turned into a star, by transforming the product concept.

When I helped to rescue Filofax in 1990 it had forfeited growth to a lower-cost rival; we stopped the firm from becoming an ex-star (and an ex-business). The concept of the organiser had evolved further, with the mass market becoming larger than the fashion retailers. Filofax was a victim of its own success, stuck in the recent past. A star that is plunging to earth is often an attractive prospect, as long as you know how to turn it back into a star.

In 1996, when my partners and I bought Plymouth Gin, it was not just as ex-star: it had almost gone to meet its Maker. But decades ago it *had* been a star, and we saw an opportunity to recreate a star in the gin market, which at that time was huge, profitable and rather drab. Astonishingly, there were only four premium gins in the world. We aimed to create the fifth, and achieve leadership in the super-premium gin market, initially in the UK and later, we hoped, throughout the world. Perhaps this was a crazy ambition, since all we committed to the venture was around £1.5 million.

We made some headway by stressing the brand's great heritage, but it was not enough. We knew that Plymouth was a unique gin with a highly distinctive taste, greatly appreciated by the experts. Our route to stardom was to raise the strength of the gin so that the taste could come through more clearly. The strategy worked beyond our wildest dreams.

The story shows that there can be surprising holes in the market, even a market as big and attractive as gin. To create your own niche, find a real consumer benefit that is currently neglected.

My fifth star, LEK Consulting, had stardom thrust upon it. We discovered that imitation couldn't lead us to stardom. We had to find a *different* route, one all our own, one that reflected our own DNA. We had to listen to what the market told us, and major on the unique products that we'd created out of desperation.

By looking at the history of my stars, I worked back to the common elements from which stardom was created.

How to create your star venture

First, you need a star idea. We've seen in detail how to create the idea, but what it boils down to is this.

★ **Invent a new niche** by dividing the existing market into two: the old, traditional market, and your new market. To be the basis for a star venture the new niche must:
  ☆ grow fast;
  ☆ be targeted at a unique set of customers or customer preferences;
  ☆ provide a different set of benefits from the main market, by doing something the main market doesn't, and by not doing some of the things the main market does;
  ☆ exhibit 'profitable variation' – provide the new product that pleases the target customers more and yet has fatter margins for your firm;
  ☆ have a clear niche name; and
  ☆ have a strong brand name that complements the niche name.

★ **To invent the new niche, get a few trusted friends together** and brainstorm ideas, using the triggers provided in Chapter 9. Develop a shortlist of possible ideas. Evaluate which idea is best.

Benefit from somebody else's star

You don't have to start a star venture to benefit from one. Instead, you can look for a 'baby star', and work or invest in it. Betfair has been by far my most profitable star, and yet I didn't invent the idea, or fund it from the start. I found a baby star a few months after it started. I knew it was a star, and pumped in as much cash as they would take.

Nor do you need money. You can benefit hugely by going to work in a baby star. If you have normal ambition and interest in work, you'll be much happier and wealthier from joining a star venture.

Although stars are rare, if you know what you are looking for it won't take you long to find your star. It just takes energy and determination.

Fake stars and non-stars

Not all ventures I thought would become stars did so. It's easy to be wrong at the ideas stage.

But, once a venture's been going for a few months, it's easy to tell a fake star. The new category doesn't turn out to be really distinct from the main market, nor does the niche grow very fast, nor does it generate a cadre of loyal customers. The new venture isn't very profitable, and doesn't look as if it ever will be.

If you work or invest in a fake star, get out and find a real one, unless you're very confident that the venture can be changed into a real star by some radical move. Reserve your energy or money for real stars.

The star takes off

For a baby star to take off, the star idea has to be translated into a business formula that works in practice. This is where the first 20 employees – the many-headed entrepreneur – prove their worth. To take off, four formulas must be mastered:

1. **the customer-attractive formula:** a proven way to get more and more loyal customers;

2. **the commercial formula:** the way to lock in fat margins;

3. **the delivery formula:** making a machine to deliver consistent, high-quality product on a large scale; and

4. **the innovation formula:** making innovation a way of life so your product is always miles ahead of those of rivals.

Form four small teams – probably a founder and two employees in each – charged with developing each formula and making it work.

Once the star has taken off, nothing – bar a major disaster or a more innovative rival – can stop it soaring higher and higher.

Evolve into a star

If you have a venture that isn't a star, that's bad, but it's not desperate. Why not try to evolve into a star? You have nothing to lose and the world to win.

★ Brainstorm possible star ideas that are close to your existing venture or capabilities.

★ Migrate your product. Make it different. Special. Something you know your customers will like. Something you can produce at low cost. Something that you can 'orchestrate', standing in the middle of a web or relationships with suppliers, doing as little as possible yourself apart from keeping contact with customers and taking their cash. Migrate to a product that will be difficult for rivals to supply.

★ Migrate your DNA. Make your firm distinctive. Create internal diversity, a unique brew. Identify a group of customers and hire people who will naturally identify with them and want to serve them brilliantly. Encourage intelligent experimentation at every level, in every way, at every time. Make it a way of life. Create a new type of firm.

★ Migrate your target customer base. End up with a unique set of customers or customer preferences, ideally suited to your products and DNA.

Evolution is wonderful. It is the root of all progress. Creating a new species of firm is the highest and most rewarding art of the entrepreneur.

The fading star

While a star, a venture is terrifically valuable. If it stops being a star, its value will plummet. An ex-star is a business tragedy.

Few insiders see it that way at the time. Typically, the risk of losing star status and the consequences are grossly underestimated. Filofax lost its star status twice and its value fell sharply both times. Betfair nearly lost its star status. If it had, shareholders would have been more than a billion pounds poorer.

Be paranoid about loss of market share to a rival. Scrutinise what is happening, recognising that most managers don't notice until it is too late. Identify why the opposition is gaining and then outflank them.

If the problem is falling market growth, try every plausible way to make the market grow fast again. If the loss of growth cannot be reversed, sell the venture before the change in its prospects is fully apparent.

Typically, a star venture's value grows rapidly. If it loses its star status, the lost opportunity is enormous. Move heaven and earth to keep your star shining.

The importance of unreasonable expectations

Stars are not like other businesses. Stars comprise fewer than 5 per cent of all businesses, yet they contribute more than 95 per cent of long-term value. Stars should not be treated the same way as other ventures. Reasonable expectations are fine for reasonably attractive businesses

– say, your typical cash cow. But stars require unreasonable expectations. Otherwise you are leaving huge piles of cash on the table.

The value of a star is determined by its growth rate and by the number of years it grows fast. Nearly everyone vastly underestimates the growth potential of stars, and the difference that high and sustained growth makes to the venture's value.

Two things follow. One, never sell a star while it's still a star. Two, ensure that it grows much faster than currently planned.

Most stars should grow at 50–100 per cent a year during their first decade, and 20–30 per cent a year thereafter. Only rarely is a baby star venture constrained by the size of the market or by competitors. Much more often, it is held back by lack of imagination and ambition. By lack of unreasonable expectations.

There are seven ways to make your star grow faster. In descending order of importance:

1. raise the target growth rate – a good rule of thumb is to double it;

2. expand geographically before rivals emerge;

3. innovate – provide new value in existing products;

4. innovate – provide new products valued by existing customers;

5. innovate – use new channels to distribute to customers;

6. innovate – find new customers similar to your existing core ones;

7. incremental acquisitions – provided there are real benefits for your existing customers.

Star ventures deserve star people. Hire people who have worked in very fast-growth firms and understand how vital it is to grow as fast as humanly possible. Hire people who understand the firm's DNA and will fit in. Hire people who are demonstrably better than your existing people. Put huge time and effort into recruitment.

Don't be afraid of conflict, especially between owners and managers. Managers can't be expected to have the interests of owners fully at heart. The bias of intelligent owners is to drive for maximum possible growth. The bias of intelligent managers is to set reasonable rather than unreasonable expectations, so that they can look good. Having launched an extremely successful venture, founders typically want to ease off the gas. They think they deserve a more congenial life. They are right. Just so long as they don't remain in charge of the firm or impede the maximum possible growth for it.

Growth is everything. All progress comes from unreasonable people holding unreasonable expectations. Star ventures desperately need unreasonable, growth-obsessed people. Why make millions when you can make megamillions? Why make a small dent in your industry when you can revolutionise it, making it a better place?

★ ★ ★

The sky is full of stars. True, the distances between them are literally astronomical. Far more of the sky is not composed of stars than is. Yet, on a clear night, away from city lights, you can always find stars.

So in business. Stars are rare. But you can find them.

Whether you're an employee, a wannabe venture leader or an investor (of grand or modest means), a star will give you a new and far richer life.

Go do it!

index

RICHISTAN

A journey through the 21st century wealth boom
and the lives of the new rich

Robert Frank • 978 0 7499 2855 1 • £7.99

**Imagine a country populated with nothing but
millionaires. Let's call it Richistan . . .**

In this riveting book, Wall Street Journal reporter Robert
Frank explores the lives and lifestyles of the new rich and
shows how this new gilded age is affecting wider society.
Profiles of 'instapreneurs' and eccentrics from the lower
and upper reaches of Richistan take us into the rarified
world of people like Ed Bazinet, who became a multimillionaire by selling miniature ceramic villages.

The influence wielded by the new rich goes far beyond
their earning power; and Frank explores the lifestyles
developing around Richistanis – butler schools, self-help
groups for people worth $10 million or more – and where
their money is going. As wealth creation becomes more
and more globalised, *Richistan* looks behind the glitz to
find the real story of new money and its impact on the
world.

'Jaw dropping' **Observer**

*'A superb travelogue of a land with its own education, health-
care and transport systems, holiday destinations and social norms,
which is anthropological in scope and not judgmental.'*
Evening Standard

*'A fascinating excursion through the lives of the rich. The rise and
rise of rich people is the most important and least noticed economic
trend of our time. Richistan is a lively glimpse of the future.'*
Richard Koch, author of *The 80/20 Principle*

THE TOP 10 HABITS OF MILLIONAIRES

Transform your thinking – and get rich

Keith Cameron Smith • 978 0 7499 2857 5 • £6.99

What does it take to become a millionaire – hard work, determination, a bit of luck? All of those help, but as entrepreneur and motivational speaker Keith Cameron Smith makes clear in this life-changing book, millionaire is first and foremost a state of mind.

In *The Top 10 Habits of Millionaires*, Smith elborates ten key principles that animate the millionaire mindset – habits that can be learned and mastered by anyone who wants to improve their financial position, including

Millionaires think long term – Create a clear vision of the life you desire and focus on it

Millionaires talk about ideas, not things and people – Ask positive 'what if' questions every day and bounce ideas off successful people who will be honest with you

Millionares embrace change – Be patient while change is unfolding and find the hidden benefit

What you believe about money has everything to do with how much money you will make. Following Keith Cameron Smith's smart and sensible advice will help you achieve long-sought financial – and emotional – abundance.

HOW COME THAT IDIOT'S RICH AND I'M NOT?

Robert Shemin • 978 0 74992867 4 • £12.99

In this provocative and entertaining book, Robert Shemin, multimillionaire and successful entrepreneur and motivational speaker, has a secret to share with you: rich people are not that smart. In fact, they're Idiots, and if you want the wealth and fulfilment you've always desired, you need to become an Idiot, too.

In *How Come That Idiot's Rich and I'm Not?*, Shemin shows how the average 'smart' person's tendency to overthink can be financially crippling, and reveals simple principles for getting and keeping spectacular wealth. Follow the 'Path of the Idiot' with Shemin and realise the mistakes that smart people invariably make: taking small steps, effectively paralysed by fear of failure, instead of acting decisively; letting vanity prevent you from admitting ignorance, instead of finding the right person to help you achieve your dreams; and generally being 'Right-side Up' in your thinking – and broke. By following Shemin's step-by-step programme, you'll be setting big goals, leaving your comfort zone, embracing the knowledge learned from failure – and reaping big rewards.

'*This book shows the average person not only how to get rich, but create, connect and contribute greatly. Open the door to a better future now by absorbing what Shemin has to say.*'
Mark Victor Hansen, co-creator of the *Chicken Soup for the Soul*® series

'*If you've spent your life doing "all the right things" but still feel like you're running in place financially, do yourself a favour and buy this book.*'
T. Harv Eker, author of *Secrets of the Millionaire Mind*

SECRETS OF THE
MILLIONAIRE MIND

Think rich to get rich

T. Harv Eker • 978 0 7499 2789 9 • £7.99

Why do some people seem to achieve wealth effortlessly while others work just as hard but still struggle financially? In this international bestselling book T. Harv Eker explains how you can master the inner game of money so that you will achieve financial success – and keep it once you have it. To get rich, you have to think rich!

Secrets of the Millionaire Mind provides a dynamic, no-nonsense programme for changing your inner model of wealth and success. Using breakthrough techniques T. Harv Eker shows how childhood and family experiences and inner mental attitudes shape your view of money. Each of us has a personal money blueprint ingrained in our subconscious minds, and it is this blueprint that will determine the course of our financial lives. Eker reveals:

• Powerful 'declarations' that drive new, money-attracting beliefs into your subconscious

• Dozens of high income and wealth-creation strategies

• What truly wealthy people know that others do not

• The cause of almost all financial problems

• How to earn passive income, so you can make money while you sleep

Armed with the insights in this book you can take action to transform your financial self quickly and permanently, starting immediately.

'If you want to learn about the root cause of success, read Secrets of the Millionaire Mind.'
Robert G. Allen, author of *The One Minute Millionaire* and *Multiple Streams of Income*

'I have admired Harv Eder's work for years and I highly recommend this book.'
Jack Canfield, co-author of *Chicken Soup for the Soul*